# "FEAR NOT! FOR BEHOLD, I BRING YOU GOOD TIDINGS OF GREAT JOY, WHICH SHALL BE TO ALL PEOPLE . . ."

Thus an angel spoke to the astonished shepherds in Bethlehem, and lit a flame of hope that nearly two thousand years have not extinguished. The story of Jesus is many things to many people. But to all it offers a message of peace and love that has never been more important and meaningful than in the modern world. Pearl Buck has retold this immortal drama in a way that gives fresh luster to its timeless beauty, and vivid focus to its eternal relevance. Here is a book for all ages, all faiths, all humankind, told with matchless artistry and glowing inspiration.

"A truly great reading experience!"
—*Chattanooga Times*

"To be appreciated by every person, no matter what his religious belief!"
—*South Bend Tribune*

"Beautifully written. . . . Pearl Buck has performed a splendid service!"
—*Philadelphia Bulletin*

*"The Bible, in both Old and New Testaments, may be read in many ways. For some it constitutes divine teaching. For others it is the purest literature we have in the English language. For still others, it is a compendium of information on suffering, struggling, rejoicing human nature."*

—PEARL S. BUCK

# The Story Bible

## Volume II  The New Testament

### by Pearl S. Buck

A SIGNET BOOK from
NEW AMERICAN LIBRARY
TIMES MIRROR

Library of Congress Catalog Card Number: 71-141871

Produced by Lyle Kenyon Engel
Editors:
Valerie Moolman
Marla Ray
George Engel

SIGNET TRADEMARK REG. U.S. PAT. OFF. AND FOREIGN COUNTRIES
REGISTERED TRADEMARK—MARCA REGISTRADA
HECHO EN CHICAGO, U.S.A.

SIGNET, SIGNET CLASSICS, MENTOR, PLUME AND MERIDIAN BOOKS
are published by The New American Library, Inc.,
1301 Avenue of the Americas, New York, New York 10019

FIRST PRINTING, JULY, 1972

6  7  8  9  10  11  12

PRINTED IN THE UNITED STATES OF AMERICA

# Contents

# Foreword

When I was a child growing up in China in the household of my American parents, I was not encouraged to read the Bible. My father, scholar in Hebrew and Greek, considered the translation of the Old and New Testaments inadequate renderings of the ancient texts and, irritated by what he considered downright mistakes in the use of words, he ignored the English version and read the Scriptures in the original languages. Since he did not teach me either Hebrew or Greek, I was reduced to English, but without encouragement I did not read the Bible. True, I heard it read for brief periods, night and morning, when my father summoned the household to family prayers. In the morning he read in English a few verses chosen by him for the benefit of his American family and in the evening he read another few verses in Chinese for the benefit of our Chinese servants. Beyond this my knowledge of the Bible was limited to the memorizing of the Beatitudes and Psalms and parts of the old prophets as Sunday occupation and to the reading—with much pleasure, I might say—of a very fat volume in a brown cloth cover entitled *Stories of the Bible* in worn gilt letters. My mother, who delighted in the English language, required me to memorize those parts of the Bible which she considered most beautiful and poetic, and to assuage my undying thirst for stories she found the fat volume for me.

Now as everyone knows who has read the Bible, there is not a better source for story than this vast collection of verse and prose, song and lamentation, love and death, sin and punishment. The scriptures of any religion are a fascinating and profound revelation of the struggle of the souls of men and women to find the source of their being and the cause of life and death. In recent years, for example, the sacred books of the Sikh religion in India have been beautifully translated into English and to my joy copies of these two volumes were presented to me on a recent trip to India. Reading them, I discover the same spiritual urgency that inspired my own youthful soul when I began to read the Bible for myself. Thus it is with other scriptures, wherever they are found. The books of Buddhism, the richly colored tales of Hinduism, the pantheons of Greece and Rome share with the Hebrew and Greek Testaments the stories of man's yearning to penetrate the Beyond. All have certain stories in common. The virgin birth is not unique to Christianity and it loses nothing of its importance thereby. The story of the great flood and Noah's ark is to be found in more than one literature. Reared as I have been in Asia, I find one religion enhances and deepens another by correlation and corroboration.

It is not as religion, however, that the stories contained in this volume are presented. I remember simply that I derived great pleasure and profit from reading that earlier volume of *Stories of the Bible*, and since I do not see its duplicate, it may be that this collection will take its place for today's readers.

The Bible, in both Old and New Testaments, may be read in many ways. For some it constitutes divine teaching, and it does contain this element. For others it is the purest literature we have in the English language. For still others it is a compendium of information on suffering, struggling, rejoicing human nature. For children, it is a story book. May they read it as I read it long ago in a Chinese house on a Chinese hillside!

Yet stay—as I write it occurs to me that the Bible

has another meaning. It is an Asian book, for Christianity came out of the East. It seems a contradiction that today the West, facing conflict with the East, should nevertheless find its own source of spiritual life in a volume of Asia, centering about the Jews, who, though they have wandered far, nevertheless remain in many ways true to their ancient history which is Asian. It may be that in this very fact we shall find the means of a common understanding, a basic agreement on the constitution for a peaceful world.

# The Story Bible

# The Angel Gabriel

✦✦✦✦✦✦✦✦✦✦✦✦✦✦✦✦✦✦✦✦✦✦✦

There was in the days of Herod, the king of Judea, a certain priest named Zacharias. He and his wife Elizabeth were both descended from Aaron, brother of Moses, and thus were both of priestly family. It happened, at this time, that Zacharias was to take his turn at serving in the temple at Jerusalem.

Now this temple was not that which had been built by Solomon, destroyed by Nebuchadnezzar, and rebuilt by the captives of the land of Judah on their return from Babylon. It was a great new temple, larger and more elaborate than ever before, and it had been built by Herod the Great to please the Jews so that they might not revolt against him and the harshness of his rule. And Herod, in his turn, was not truly the King of the Jews but the governor of the province of Judah or Judea, which was one fourth part of the whole land of Palestine. Each part had its own king or governor, and all four rulers were responsible to Caesar Augustus, emperor in Rome and powerful ruler of all the lands in the region of the Mediterranean Sea. Little Palestine was the smallest part of the great Caesar's mighty empire. Yet it was a very much larger land than it had been in the days of Nehemiah, it was much more thickly populated, and it was more advanced in many ways. The Jews had learned much from the learned Greeks and conquering Romans, but they had not learned to free themselves from foreign rule. One day, they were sure, a leader would be born among them, a man of God who would save them from their sins and from their earthly bondage. He would be the one true King of the Jews: the Messiah, he who would deliver them, and the Christ, he who would be the anointed of the Lord. The prophets of old had assured them that their Savior would come.

And still the Jews were waiting.

In the meanwhile they prayed. Those who were deeply dedicated to the God of Israel made frequent pilgrimages to the city of Jerusalem to celebrate the feasts and holy days with the priests and wise men of the temple. Those who lived in Jerusalem worshiped in the temple whenever the spirit came upon them. There was always a priest in attendance at the altar.

One day Zacharias went as usual into the inner sanctuary of the house of the Lord to burn incense upon the altar. Great crowds of people were praying outside in the temple court as he went about his priestly duties in the holiest of all the holy rooms.

Now Zacharias and Elizabeth loved the Lord and served him with all their hearts, but like so many upright and faithful people before them, they had one great cause for sorrow. They were old, and yet they had no child. If there was any one thing that they prayed for more than anything else, it was for a son of their own.

Zacharias lit the tiny flame upon the altar. The sweet smell of incense rose in a cloud of smoke. And suddenly an angel of the Lord appeared on the right side of the altar of incense. When Zacharias saw this sudden apparition he was greatly startled and troubled in his heart. He felt afraid, and he bowed his head.

"Fear not," said the angel gently. "Your prayer is

answered. Your wife Elizabeth will have a son, and you will name him John. He shall bring you joy and gladness; and many will rejoice at his birth, for he shall be great in the sight of the Lord. He will drink neither wine nor strong drink and, filled with the Holy Spirit, he will turn many of the children of Israel to the Lord their God. His spirit and power shall be that of Elijah, so that he will go before the Lord and turn the hearts of the fathers to the children, who are without sin, and the disobedient to the wisdom of the just. Thus he will make ready a people prepared to meet the Lord."

Zacharias was full of wonderment. "How can this be?" he asked. "How shall I know that this is true? For my wife and I are old, too old to have a child."

And the angel answered: "I am Gabriel, who stands in the presence of God. The Lord has sent me to you to tell you these glad tidings. But because you do not believe my words, which nevertheless will be fulfilled when the right time comes, you shall be dumb and not able to speak until the day that these things shall be performed. Let that be your sign that what I say is true."

Zacharias looked again but the angel was no longer there. The people in the temple court outside waited for the priest, wondering why he stayed so long within the inner sanctuary. When at last the old man came out his lips were moving silently and his hands made gestures in the air as if he had been taken with a sudden illness. As they stared at him, astonished, they became aware that some strange and wonderful thing had happened to him. All he could do was beckon to them dumbly and make signs that he had lost his speech, yet on his face there was a radiance that they had never seen before. It came to them, then, that he must have seen a vision in the temple, and they were filled with awe. They waited for some time to see what else might happen or what he might say when he regained his voice, but there was no sign. The old man remained speechless for all the time they waited, until at last they went away and forgot what they had seen.

When Zacharias was finished with his days of duty in the temple he departed to his own house in the rolling hills of Judea. He still could not speak, nor did he speak for several months thereafter. But soon after he came home his wife Elizabeth told him that they were, at last, to have a child.

"Thus has the Lord dealt with me after these many years!" she said joyfully. And the old man gave thanks in the silence of his heart.

Six months later the angel Gabriel appeared again. This time the messenger of the Lord came to the city of Nazareth in Galilee, in the lakelands north of the province of Judea, and visited the maiden Mary who was betrothed to a carpenter named Joseph. Now Mary was cousin to Elizabeth, but she had heard nothing of the vision to Zacharias in the temple. Nor did she herself plan to marry her intended husband for some time to come, though all their friends and kinsfolk felt that she and Joseph had done well to choose each other. It was good, they said among themselves, that both Mary and Joseph were descended from the house of David, he who had once been king of all Israel.

It was a quiet day in Nazareth for Mary until the unexpected figure came to her as if from nowhere. And she looked up in surprise at the calm face of the stranger.

"Hail, Mary, you who are highly favored!" said the angel Gabriel. "The Lord is with you: blessed are you among all women!"

When Mary saw this sudden visitor, she was deeply troubled. What could this greeting mean? She could not understand it, and she trembled at his words.

"Fear not, Mary," the angel said to her, "for you have found favor with the Lord your God. You shall have a son, and you will call him Jesus. He shall be great, and shall be called the Son of the Highest. The Lord God will give him the throne of his forefather

David, and he will reign over the house of Israel forever. Of his kingdom there shall be no end."

Mary was astonished and even more troubled, for her wedding day was still far off and Joseph was no king to be father to a king. "How can this be?" she asked the angel. "I am not yet married, and the man I am to marry is a good man but a carpenter. How then shall our son be king?"

"The Holy Ghost will come upon you," Gabriel answered. "The power of the Most High God shall cover you, therefore the holy child that will be born to you shall be called the Son of God. And behold! Your cousin Elizabeth is soon to have a child of her old age. For with God, nothing is impossible."

When she heard this Mary believed and no longer feared. "I am the handmaid of the Lord," she said humbly. "Let it be to me as you have said."

And the angel departed from her as suddenly as he had come.

Yet the news was so startling to Mary that she could not bring herself to tell it to her parents, nor to the man she was to marry. She therefore arose in haste and went into the hill country of Judea to visit her cousin Elizabeth.

Strangely enough, Elizabeth was not surprised to see her, for when Mary greeted her the older woman was filled with the Holy Spirit and the knowledge that came with it. She cried out in a joyous voice: "Blessed are you among women! Blessed am I that the mother of my Lord should come to me! And blessed is she that believes, for indeed those things will happen which were promised by the Lord!"

So Elizabeth already knew! Mary answered with joy in her own heart:

"Oh, how my soul does magnify the Lord,
And my spirit does rejoice in God my Savior.
For he has taken notice of his handmaiden in her
   lowly estate;

Behold, from henceforth all generations shall call
me blessed.
For he that is mighty has done to me great things,
And holy is his name!
And his mercy is on those who love him from
generation to generation.
He has showed strength with his arm;
He has scattered the proud in the imagination of
their hearts.
He has thrown down the mighty from their seats
of power,
And has lifted up those of low degree.
He has filled the hungry with good things,
And the rich he has sent empty away.
He has helped his servant Israel, in remembrance
of his mercy,
As he spoke to our fathers, to Abraham, and to
his children forever!"

Mary stayed with Elizabeth for about three months,
helping her cousin as the older woman grew heavy with
the child, and when the little one was born she returned
to her own home in Nazareth with the knowledge that
she, too, was to have a baby.

When Elizabeth brought forth her son, her friends
and family gathered around to rejoice with her. The
Lord had indeed shown great mercy to the wife of
Zacharias! And on the eighth day after the birth they
came to sanctify the child and offer suggestions for his
name.

"Let him be called Zacharias, after his father," they
said.

But Elizabeth shook her head and answered: "Not
so. He shall be called John."

Now this was most surprising to them. "But there is
no one in your family by the name of John," they
argued. "Why do you not name him for your husband?" And they made signs to the father, who was

still incapable of speech, to ask him what he desired to name his son.

Zacharias motioned for a writing tablet. When they brought it to him he wrote these words upon it: "His name is John."

And they marveled, all of them; yet they marveled even more when suddenly his mouth was opened and his tongue was loosed.

The power of speech came back to him and he praised God with all his new-found eloquence. He was filled with the Holy Ghost, and he prophesied, and said:

"Blessed be the Lord God of Israel!
For he has visited and redeemed his people,
And has raised up a horn of salvation for us
In the house of his servant David,
As he spoke by the mouths of his holy prophets
Which have been since the world began:
That we should be saved from our enemies,
And from the hand of all that hate us;
To perform the mercy promised to our fathers,
And to remember his holy covenant,
The oath which he swore to our father Abraham!"

Fear came on all the people who heard him and on those who lived round about when they heard their neighbors repeat the words of Zacharias. "What manner of child is this?" they wondered to each other, and remembered the words within their hearts.

But Zacharias had no doubts about his child. He knew that the hand of the Lord was with him. And to the baby John, even before the little one could understand, he said:

"And you, my child, shall be called the prophet of
    the Highest,
For you will go before the face of the Lord to pre-
    pare his ways;
To give knowledge of salvation to his people

By the forgiving of their sins
Through the tender mercy of our God;
To give light to them that sit in darkness and in
the shadow of death,
And to guide our feet into the way of peace."

And the child grew, and became strong in body and spirit. When he was of an age to leave his home he went into the desert where he fasted, studied the holy writings, and prayed until the day when he was ready to preach to the children of Israel.

In the meanwhile Mary had gone home to her parents and the man, Joseph, who was to be her husband. It was strange to him that she was already carrying a child within her although she was still a maiden and unmarried, but she told him all that she had seen and heard.

And one night, while he was thinking about all the strange things she had told him, Joseph fell into a restless sleep. An angel of the Lord appeared to him in a dream and said to him: "Joseph, son of David! Fear not for Mary's sake, or for your own for she has been visited by the Holy Ghost, the Spirit of the Most High. She will have a son and you shall call him Jesus, for he shall be the Savior of his people."

Joseph awoke, untroubled and refreshed in spirit. Soon afterward he took the maiden Mary to be his wife, and they lived together in Nazareth awaiting the birth of the baby who was to be called Jesus.

Elizabeth and Zacharias knew that their son John was to be a prophet preparing the way for a greater man than himself. And Mary and Joseph had been told that the boy Jesus was of his people. The young couple and the old looked forward with great eagerness to the days to come.

# The Birth of Jesus

❋❋❋❋❋❋❋❋❋❋❋❋❋❋❋❋❋❋❋❋❋❋❋❋

One day a proclamation was made throughout the land of Palestine and all the vast number of territories under the dominion of the Roman emperor. It said: "It is decreed by Caesar Augustus that a record shall be made of all the people in his possessions and lands so that each one may be taxed according to his property. Every man must place his name upon the tax list in the city of his fathers, from whence his family came."

Therefore every person in the land of the Hebrews, Roman subjects like so many hundreds of thousands of people throughout the world, went to his own city to put his name upon a register and pay his tax.

For Joseph and Mary, both of whom were of the house and family of David who had been born in Bethlehem, it meant a journey of seventy miles from Nazareth in Galilee to Bethlehem in southern Judea. Joseph was much displeased to have to travel at that time, for Mary his wife was soon to have her child. But they were obliged by law to go, and there was no delaying.

Mary made no complaint and they set off at once. Joseph walked by her side as she rode upon a slowly jogging mule along the rough road to the south. It was a long and tiring journey, and by the time they reached the town of Bethlehem six miles south of Jerusalem the place was already crowded with other citizens who had come to register their names upon the tax rolls. Crowds jostled through the narrow streets seeking lodgings for the night; people pushed their way into the only inn and begged for rooms in the private houses; and no one gave any thought to the plight of the carpenter from Nazareth and his wife who was so soon to have a child.

And because there was no room for them in the inn they sought shelter in a stable, making beds for themselves amongst the sweet-smelling straw in a clean and quiet corner that was separate from the animal stalls. Joseph made Mary as comfortable as he could on a soft blanket of hay, and then he looked about to see what else he might do to improve their simple shelter. There was the child to think of; it would need some sort of bed. He found a manger, one of the troughs from which the livestock ate their fodder, cleaned it out with care and prepared it as best he could for the coming of the child.

And so it was, while they were there in Bethlehem by order of an emperor in far-off Rome, that it came time for Mary to deliver her child. There in the stable she brought forth her firstborn son and wrapped him tenderly in swaddling clothes; and Joseph placed the baby gently in the manger he had so lovingly prepared.

The sun had set some hours before and the little town was very quiet. Bright stars flecked the cloudless sky above the sleeping folk in Bethlehem, and only in the fields nearby were there men who stood awake and watchful. They were shepherds, keeping watch over their flocks by night so that no wolves or thieves might come upon their sheep and carry even one away. Sometimes they were silent, and sometimes they talked, but at no time did they relax their guard over the least among their lambs. It was a calm night, bright and peaceful; too bright for anything to happen that might endanger the flock.

Then all at once it was even brighter than before: a great and wonderful light filled the sky, and the brilliant glory of the Lord shone round about the shepherds so dazzlingly, so suddenly, that their hearts leapt within them and they quaked with fear. And an angel appeared before them in the brilliance and cried out a message that brought them to their knees in prayer:

"Fear not! For behold, I bring you good tidings of great joy, which shall be to all people. For unto you is born this day in the city of David a Savior, which is Christ the Lord. And this shall be a sign to you: You will find the babe wrapped in swaddling clothes, lying in a manger."

The light that streamed down from the sky grew brighter yet, and suddenly there was with the angel a multitude of heavenly beings. They shone, themselves, in the brightness above the fields; and as the shepherds watched and listened with awe the heavenly choir praised God and sang:

"Glory to God in the highest, and on earth peace, goodwill toward men."

Then they were gone from the shepherds, away into the heavens, and the radiant light faded into the ordinary brightness of a cloudless, starry night. The shepherds rose in wonder and stared at one another.

"Let us go at once to Bethlehem," they said, "and see for ourselves this thing that has come to pass which the Lord has made known to us."

They went with haste, marveling at all they had seen and heard, and sought out the stable near the inn. There they found Mary and Joseph, and the newborn babe lying sleeping in the manger. And they knelt before the wondrous child of whom the angels had spoken, and they told Mary about the angelic host that had come to them. Then they left, and in their great wonder and excitement they told all they met about the awesome events of the night. And all who heard their story wondered, and talked of it among themselves. But Mary kept within her heart all the things she knew and all that she had heard, and she pondered them in silence as she tenderly watched over the baby in the manger.

The shepherds went back to their flocks, glorifying and praising God for all the things that they had heard and seen; and thanking him for sending them a Savior, who was Christ their Lord.

On the eighth day after the birth of the child, Mary and Joseph took him to be sanctified and named. As the angel had instructed them, they called him Jesus, a name meaning "salvation."

Now when Jesus was born in Bethlehem of Judea in the days of Herod the king, there were certain wise and noble men who lived in a distant country of the east and studied the stars. One night they saw a great new star appear in the eastern sky and blaze a path across the heavens toward the kingdom of Judea, where it disappeared from sight. Being learned men, they had heard of the prophecies that had been made among the Jewish people in a day long past, and when they saw the new star they felt at once that a great new king had been born in the land of the Jews.

"Come, let us go at once to see the newborn king!" they exclaimed to one another.

They loaded their camels with gifts for the wonderful child and set off on their long journey. And because Jerusalem was known to be the holy city of the Jews, the wise men from the east traveled to that famous city of kings believing that they would find the child in some royal palace there.

When they arrived they inquired of the people: "Where is he that is born King of the Jews? For we have seen his star in the east and have come to worship him."

But no one in Jerusalem had heard of the newborn "king" who was in Bethlehem.

When Herod the king heard of their questions he

was deeply troubled, and all Jerusalem with him. After all, was Herod not King of the Jews? What child could claim his royal title? Then he too, remembered the old prophecies, and sent for the chief priests and the scribes whose duty it was to record and interpret the teachings of the past.

"Now tell me," he demanded, "where this Christ, this new king of Israel, is supposed to have been born?"

"In Bethlehem of Judea, O King Herod," they replied, "for thus it is written by the prophet:

"'And you, Bethlehem, in the land of Judah,
Are not the least among the princes of Judah:
For out of you shall come a Governor,
That shall rule my people Israel.'"

Herod sent his priests and scribes away and thought about these sayings for some time. He did not like what they might mean to him. For he was king, and king he intended to remain no matter who was born in Bethlehem or anywhere else.

After a while he sent for the wise men of the east who were inquiring within his city about the newborn King of Jews. And he sent for them in secret, for he did not want his own priests and scribes to know what they might say to him. They came to him at once, thinking that he would surely be able to tell them what they asked.

Herod asked the first question.

"Tell me," he said genially, and with unfeigned interest, "what time did this new star appear in the eastern sky?"

They told him.

"And where is it now?" he asked them cunningly.

But they did not know.

"Then go to Bethlehem," he answered, "and search there diligently for the young child, for according to the scribes that is where he may be found. But no one knows where he is in the city, therefore I beg that when you have found him you will bring me word so that I may go and worship him also."

The wise men left Jerusalem and went upon their way to Bethlehem. Herod began at once to make his plans. It was true that he desired earnestly to know where the child might be, but not so that he himself might go and worship him. It was his own throne of which he was thinking.

The star which the wise men had seen in the east appeared again before them and led them on to Bethlehem. When they saw the star once more they rejoiced with great gladness in their hearts, knowing that they were soon to see the glorious child. When the star stopped above a humble dwelling place, they went in. All they saw was a simple carpenter and his wife Mary, and a child in Mary's arms. Yet they knew at once that the baby Jesus was the newborn king they had come so far to see, for the star was still hovering over the house where the young child was. In the fullness of their joy they bent down low and worshiped him, this child who would be not only King but Savior, and when they had done worshiping they opened up their sacks and chests of treasure. They gave the child gifts worthy of a king: gold for his earthly wealth, sweet frankincense and myrrh for sacrificial offerings to the Lord God of heaven; and they gave these precious things with wonder and thanksgiving in their hearts.

When they had blessed the child and given their gifts, the wise men thought it time to return to the city of Jerusalem and tell King Herod where this wondrous child might be found and worshiped by all the people of the land. But in a dream that came to all of them that night, God's angel warned them that they should not return to Herod with their news. Therefore they left Bethlehem, avoided Jerusalem, and went back to their country by another route.

Soon after the wise men had left, the angel of the

Lord appeared to Joseph in a dream. "Arise," the angel said. "Take the young child and his mother and flee into Egypt for your safety: for Herod will seek the young child to destroy him."

Joseph arose at once in the night and gathered together the few possessions of his small family and the gifts brought by the wise men from the east. Swiftly, and in silence, he took the baby and its mother from Bethlehem by night and journeyed with all haste to the land of Egypt. And there the baby Jesus remained in safety while Herod lived out his last terrible months in the land of Judea.

King Herod waited for the wise men, but they did not come back. With growing impatience he watched for their return, waiting and yearning for their news so that he might find the child and rid himself of this threat to his kingdom; but still there was no sign of the wise men of the east. And then at last he heard that they had gone back to their own land without first coming back to him. Herod's anger knew no bounds. He knew he could not touch the wise men, but there was something he could do to destroy the child.

With the awful cruelty for which he was well known, he sent his soldiers out to Bethlehem and the surrounding countryside with orders to kill every child two years old and under. In this way he felt certain he would slay the one he wanted, in company with all those born at the time when the wise men saw the star.

His soldiers followed his terrible command. And after they had done so another prophecy of the prophet Jeremiah's was fulfilled:

"In Rama was there a voice heard,
Lamentation, and weeping, and great mourning,
Rachel weeping for her children,
And would not be comforted,
Because they are no more."

And they were no more, the children of Bethlehem who were two years old and younger. Only the baby Jesus was safe from Herod's senseless slaughter. Thus he, a child who was to be the Christ, the Savior, the Messiah of the Jewish people, began his life in a humble stable in Bethlehem and was now in hiding with his parents in the land of Egypt.

# The Boyhood of Jesus

✳✳✳✳✳✳✳✳✳✳✳✳✳✳✳✳✳✳✳✳✳✳✳✳

The boy Jesus lived. King Herod died: old, sick in body and spirit, cruel to the last.

Then the angel of the Lord appeared again in a dream to Joseph, still in Egypt with Mary and her son. "Arise," the angel said. "Take the young child and his mother back into the land of Israel, for he who sought the young child's life is dead."

So Joseph arose and led his family back to their homeland. Egypt had been good to them, as it had been good to his forefathers Abraham and Joseph, but it was not meant that the King and Deliverer of Israel should grow up in a foreign land. It was toward Bethlehem, city of David, that the family now turned their steps.

Yet there were still obstacles in Joseph's path. When he came with Mary and Jesus into the land of Israel he heard that Herod's son Archelaus reigned in Judea in his father's place, and by all accounts the son was no less cruel than the father. Therefore Joseph was afraid to settle in Judea as he had intended, and while he wondered what to do he was told by God in a dream that he must turn aside from Judea and go

29

north into the lakelands of Galilee. There another Herod ruled, one Herod Antipas, who was by no means a good and upright man but neither was he nearly so cruel as others of his family.

And so Joseph went back to the city of Nazareth in Galilee with Mary his wife and the little boy Jesus, and stayed there while the child was growing up. Thus another prophecy of old was fulfilled: "He that is the Messiah shall be called a Nazarene."

Joseph once again became a carpenter. Mary made a new home for the little family in Nazareth. The child Jesus grew, becoming strong in spirit and filled with wisdom, and the grace of God was upon him.

As time passed and the boy seemed to be no different from others of his age, Mary and Joseph thought less and less of the strange circumstances of his birth. They did not, and could not ever, forget, but he gave them no reason to treat him as anything other than a normal, healthy lad with all the usual interests of a growing boy.

Yet he was wiser than they knew, and nothing that he saw escaped him. As Jesus grew he came to know his town and everything about it, good and bad. He knew its people, old and young; its rich men and its poor, the kind people and the harsh, the tradesmen and the beggars. In his father's shop he learned much about the use of tools and the differences between various kinds of wood. And because a carpenter of those days was as much a builder as a maker of furniture, he also came to know something of the construction of houses. The boy Jesus could only watch when it came to the matter of building, but he was quick to learn the importance of a solid foundation, sturdy materials, and honest workmanship.

And because Nazareth was not a large town he also came to know the countryside around him as if it were the garden of his father's house. He knew the shores of Galilee and the fishermen who went out to cast their nets upon the waters. He knew the shepherds of the pastures, and came to share their feeling of concern and love for every lamb in every flock. He knew the farmers in the fields, and he watched them plow and reap. He knew the names of all the living things that grew in the hills and valleys: the crops, the trees, the fruits, the mustard seeds and weeds. He knew the birds and beasts and flowers, the thorns and thistles, and the grasses of the fields.

He also learned the history of his people and the commandments brought down by Moses from the top of Mount Sinai. Although the temple was in Jerusalem, and all devout Jews journeyed there for their special prayers and feasts, there was a synagogue in Nazareth where the people gathered for worship and to hear readings from the scrolls of wisdom left by the Hebrew prophets and poets of the past. Here in the synagogue Jesus praised the Lord on sabbath days, and here he studied the psalms and scriptures during the week until he could recite long passages by heart. Here, too, he learned to read and write, and to understand the words of wisdom that he had learned by listening to his teachers. Time and time again he heard the hopeful prophecies about the Messiah who would come to free his people Israel from the darkness of their own sins and the yoke of their oppressors. The yearning for yet more knowledge and understanding began to stir within him.

In accordance with the custom among the Jewish people, Joseph and Mary went to Jerusalem every year to celebrate the feast of the passover. And when Jesus was twelve years old his parents took him with them for the first time, for now he was on the verge of young manhood.

There was much for Jesus to see on the journey to the city of the temple, and much to interest him in the great city itself as crowds of pilgrims converged upon it from all sides. But it was the temple itself that stirred him more than the royal palace, the markets with their many wares, the noblemen in all their finery, or the impressive soldiers of the king. Instead of lingering in the streets with other boys his age he went each day to the temple and listened to the priests, and each evening he joined his parents as they praised the Lord and worshiped the Most High. He was fascinated by the altar and the sweet smell of burning incense, by the calm-faced priests in their flowing robes, and by the compelling words of the wise teachers within the temple court.

The feast of the lamb and the unleavened bread was celebrated by all, and much too soon the days of special prayers and fasts and feasts were at an end. The pilgrims who were going back to Nazareth gathered in a great company so that they might travel the long road together, and they set off from the city of Jerusalem in one vast but scattered throng.

But the child Jesus stayed behind in Jerusalem, unable to tear himself away and not even aware that his parents were already far distant while he sat listening and questioning in the temple. Strange new thoughts were working in his mind. He had been told the story of his birth, and more than once he thought of the words of one of the earliest of the ancient prophets:

"There shall come forth a star out of Jacob,
And a scepter shall rise out of Israel."

Was his the star? He could only wonder. But in his heart there was a feeling that the God of Israel was his Father and that he, the Son, had much to learn.

Joseph and Mary did not know that Jesus was not with them, for the group they traveled with was large and Jesus might have been anywhere within it with his young friends or his relatives. At the end of a day's journey they looked for him so that he might join them as they made camp for the night, and then at last they realized that he was nowhere to be seen. With growing anxiety they sought him among their kinsfolk and acquaintances, but they did not find him nor anyone who could tell them where he was. It came to them, then, that perhaps he had not left the city.

They hurried back at once and searched throughout the city, looking in all the places where they thought a young boy might have wandered. But still they did not find him, and their desperate questions met with no answer that could help them. No one had seen the boy.

And then, after three days spent in traveling and in searching, they went into the temple. And there they found their child sitting in the midst of the doctors and the learned scribes. He was listening to them with rapt attention and asking questions that showed so deep a knowledge and understanding that all who heard him were astounded. Both his questions and his answers showed a wisdom well beyond his years, and the learned men were talking to him almost as if he were one of them.

Joseph and Mary were themselves amazed, as much by his presence there as by his remarkable understanding. At the moment they were in no mood to congratulate their son upon his wisdom.

His mother said to him: "Son, why have you treated us this way? Did you not know that we were all to leave together? Your father and I have been seeking for you in sorrow, afraid that we might never find you."

He looked at them with surprise. "But I am in my Father's house. Why did you seek me? Did you not know that I must be about my Father's business?"

His parents did not understand. His father's business? What could he mean?

When Jesus saw that he had saddened them he rose at once and left the temple with them. Yet Mary grew thoughtful as they resumed their journey. Though the years had dimmed her memory of the visit of the angel, she had not forgotten that her son was no ordinary boy. Meanwhile Jesus went back to Nazareth with Joseph and Mary. From that time on, throughout his youth and early manhood, he was obedient to them in every way and never again gave them cause for hurt or sorrow.

But Mary thought often about the words he had used that day in the temple at Jerusalem: "Why did you seek me? Did you not know that I must be about my Father's business?"

And Jesus increased in wisdom as he grew in stature. As the years went by he grew in favor with both God and man. He lived a quiet life in Nazareth and gave no further sign that he was anything other than the son of a hard-working carpenter, except that he was perhaps more gentle and forgiving than most men and certainly more wise. To all who knew him then he was a kindly, ordinary Nazarene.

But his time was coming.

# John the Baptist

✠✠✠✠✠✠✠✠✠✠✠✠✠✠✠✠✠✠✠✠✠✠✠✠

The cousins John and Jesus grew to manhood, John in Judea and Jesus in the land of Galilee. In Rome, the emperor Augustus died. In Jerusalem, the cruel Archelaus was replaced as king of Judea by a procurator, or governor, named Pontius Pilate. Herod Antipas was still the tetrarch or royal administrator of Galilee; and Annas and Caiaphas were high priests of the temple in Jerusalem.

Now in the fifteenth year of the rule of the emperor Tiberius, when both John and Jesus were about thirty years old, John the son of Elizabeth and Zacharias left the desert country of his childhood and went into the wilderness to preach. The word of God came to him in the wild hill country of Judea, and he knew that his mission was to spread the word to all the people he could reach.

There were in Palestine, at that time, two main Jewish sects who worshiped the God of Israel with a great show of outward fervor. These were the Pharisees and the Sadducees, who were much alike in many ways. The essential difference between the two parties was that the Pharisees believed not only in the written

Laws of Moses but also in laws and traditions that had been handed down by word of mouth, while the Sadducees, who were the priestly aristocracy, rejected all doctrines but those of the written Law. Both parties were powerful in the temple, both were deeply occupied with the rituals and ceremonies of their religion, and both were more concerned with strict observance of the letter of the Mosaic Law than with the spirit of it. They practiced all the rites with the utmost care, and they prayed all the required prayers with the greatest diligence; and in doing so they firmly believed that they were fulfilling all their obligations to God. But they were blinded by the trappings of their beliefs, and they forgot that godliness includes the everyday practice of neighborliness and love. In them there was more pride than faith, more knowledge of the outward form of their religion than understanding of its meaning.

John belonged to neither of these two sects. He cared nothing for rituals and formal prayers. His only concern was to pave the way for the coming Messiah, whoever he might be and whenever he might come, by persuading people to repent of their sins and turn their hearts to God.

And so he went into the country near the Jordan River, preaching; urging men to be baptized, to confess, to repent, to save themselves through sincere repentance, to prepare for the day when God would judge them according to their deeds on earth. It was John of whom the Lord God had spoken through the prophet Isaiah, saying:

"Behold, I send thy messenger before thy face,
Which shall prepare the way before thee;
The voice of one crying in the wilderness,
'Prepare ye the way of the Lord!
Make his paths straight.
Every valley shall be filled,
And every mountain and hill shall be brought low;
And the crooked shall be made straight,

And the rough ways shall be made smooth;
And all flesh shall see the salvation of God.' "

People came from far and wide to see this man who baptized in the Jordan and to hear his words. Among them were simple folk from the countryside of Judea, rich men from the towns, and scholars from the city of Jerusalem. With a zeal and fervor unmatched by any temple priest, John preached his message of repentance to all those who came to him. They confessed their sins and let him baptize them as a symbol of their cleansing; and they stared at him and wondered who he was.

He was like no one they had ever seen or heard before. His clothing was a robe of camel's hair with a leather cord about the waist, and his food was locusts and wild honey. He did not speak of the small, intricate details of the Law that were so important to the learned temple scribes, nor did he speak of altars, incense, or burnt offerings. His eyes burned with the light of earnestness as his tongue spoke strange words of a much greater Light that was to come, of a Being who would bring his listeners grace and truth and hope, of a Christ that was even now upon the earth.

Word of him continued to spread throughout the land. People told each other that a new prophet had come—a new Elijah, or perhaps even the long-awaited Messiah himself.

The Pharisees sent priests and Levites from Jerusalem to question him. They, too, marveled at his strangeness and his sayings.

"Who are you?" they asked. "Are you the Christ?"

"I am not the Christ," he answered.

"Who are you, then? Are you Elijah, returned to Israel?"

"No, I am not," he said.

"Or some other prophet? Tell us who you are, so that we may give an answer to those who sent us. What do you say of yourself?"

And he answered, "I am the voice of one crying in the wilderness, he of whom Isaiah spoke."

"Why do you baptize, then," they asked, "if you are not the Christ, or Elijah the prophet?"

"To prepare for another who is to come," he answered. "For there is one coming who is mightier than I, whose shoestrings I am not worthy to stoop down and unloose. I have indeed baptized with water, but he shall baptize with the Holy Spirit and with fire!"

And the people kept on coming to him, to be baptized in the Jordan and confess their sins. He was glad when they came, but he was angry when he saw Pharisees and Sadducees among the crowds. To him, they were hypocrites: righteous, zealous, self-denying on the surface, but self-righteous in their hearts and smugly certain that they had no need for baptism and repentance.

He looked at them and cried out angrily: "You brood of snakes! Who has warned you to come to me so that you might flee from the wrath to come? Bring forth deeds that show your true repentance! Do not boast and say to yourselves, 'We have Abraham for our father,' and think that that is enough to save you. For I say to you that God is able to raise up children for Abraham from these very stones! Therefore, what are you? And I tell you now that the axe is ready at the roots of the trees, to cut down those which do not bring forth good fruit. And they shall be cut down and cast into the fire! Repent, show good deeds while there is time."

The priests and Pharisees, the Sadducees and scribes, were outraged by John's words. But many people were moved and wanted to know what they should do to show their repentance.

"Give," he said. "He that has two coats, let him give one to a man who had none. And he that has more food than he needs, let him do the same."

Then there came also certain publicans, or tax collectors, to be baptized by John. They were among the most hated of men, for the law permitted them to extort as much money as they could out of their fellow Jews and keep for themselves any sum above that which was required by the Roman emperor. Many, though not all of them, were cruel and greedy beyond words, and the Jews regarded them as the worst of sinners.

And when the tax collectors came to John they said to him:

"Master, what shall we do to show ourselves worthy of forgiveness?"

"Exact no more than that which is appointed to you," answered John.

"And what shall we do?" asked the soldiers.

"Do violence to no man," said John. "Make no false accusations. And be content with your wages, instead of taking money in dishonest ways."

Thus did John baptize and preach and answer all their questions. Dozens, scores, and hundreds of people declared themselves his followers, and yet they did not know what to make of him. They wondered in their hearts whether John might not really be the Christ. Again they asked.

Again John answered: "No! But there is one among you, whom you do not recognize for what he is. He is the one who, coming after me, will be preferred before me. It is he who will baptize you with fire. His winnowing fork is in his hand, and he will clean his threshing floor. The wheat he will gather into his granary, but the chaff he will burn up with unquenchable fire. Will you be wheat? Or will you be chaff? Repent, I say to you!"

There were many other warnings he gave to the people who came to listen to him. No one was spared his warning words or the wrath of his rough tongue. Wherever he saw evil, he pointed at it and denounced it, no matter what the cost might be to him. Not even Herod escaped John's outspoken criticism. For Herod Antipas, tetrarch or governor of Galilee, had married his own brother Philip's wife. No common citizen would have gone unpunished for this crime, but no one dared to speak against a king. No one, that is, but John. John said whatever he wished about Herod's various crimes, particularly his illegal marriage.

Miles away in Galilee, Herod heard of this man whom other men were calling John the Baptist.

Jesus also heard of his cousin's work. Unlike Herod, he left Galilee and went to Jordan to be baptized by John. He had not yet begun to preach himself, but now his time was come and he was ready.

John looked at him as he came, and perceived something that other men did not yet know and many more men would never believe. And when Jesus asked his cousin John to baptize him as he baptized all others who came to him, John at first refused him, saying: "It is I who need to be baptized by you. And do you come to me?"

And Jesus answered, saying, "It is fitting that we should do all righteous things."

Then John led him into the river and baptized him.

When Jesus had been baptized he rose up from the water, and as he did so the heavens opened above him and he saw the Spirit of God coming down like a dove to rest upon him. He heard a voice from heaven saying: "This is my beloved Son, in whom I am well pleased."

John saw the Spirit descending as a dove out of heaven and alighting upon Jesus. He knew, then, that Jesus was the Son of God.

And Jesus himself knew without a doubt that he had been born of God and appointed by God to be the Savior of his people.

# Jesus
## in the Wilderness

✠✠✠✠✠✠✠✠✠✠✠✠✠✠✠✠✠✠✠✠✠✠✠

After Jesus had been baptized he left Jordan and was led deep into the wilderness by the Spirit of God to be tempted by the devil. He was certain now that he was to spend the rest of his life doing God's work, but he felt the need to be alone with his own thoughts and test his own resolve. Difficult days lay ahead, and he wanted to think and pray in a quiet place before beginning his teaching mission.

For forty days and forty nights he fasted in the wilderness. And when the long days and nights had passed he was weak with hunger. The voice of the devil spoke in his mind.

"If you are indeed the Son of God," whispered the voice of the tempter, "why do you not command that these stones be made into bread?"

Jesus looked at the stones lying on the hillside, knowing that he could indeed turn them into bread if he so desired. But the divine power at his command had not been intended for his own satisfaction, nor was the provision of food for the hungry his major mission on earth. It was spiritual food that he was destined to provide.

"It is written," he answered, "that man shall not live by bread alone, but by the word of God."

And then it was as if the devil had led him to the holy city, and set him on the spire of the temple.

"If you are the Son of God," the voice said temptingly, "God will let no harm come to you. Cast yourself down from this height; show a great sign so that all may believe in you. For it is written that God will put you in the care of his angels to keep you from harm. In their hands will they bear you up, so that you shall not so much as strike your foot against a stone."

It would indeed have been a wonderful sign to all people. Such a miracle would surely make them wonder and listen to his words; they would have no doubt that Jesus had been sent by God. But it was not God's way, nor the way of Jesus, to convince people with spectacular signs. They must receive him because they loved God and believed in him, and not because they were impressed by wondrous signs.

"It is so written," Jesus agreed. "And it is also written: 'You shall not tempt the Lord thy God.'"

Again the devil took him up onto a high mountain to show him a vision of the kingdoms of the world and the glory of them.

"All these things will I give you," said the tempter, "and all the power and the glory of them. For all is mine, to give to whomsoever I choose. If you will fall down and worship me, it will all be yours."

But Jesus did not want earthly power and glory, for his was the kingdom of heaven. True, with his great powers, he was capable of taking possession of the entire world. But God's kingdom could not be shown to people by the tempter's way; it could only be shown by teaching them to love and serve and worship.

Then Jesus answered: "Get thee behind me, Satan! For it is written: 'You shall worship the Lord your God, and only him shall you serve.'"

At last the devil left him. After forty days and nights in the wilderness, tempted by Satan and with only the wild beasts for company, Jesus finished wrestling with his thoughts. And the angels came and ministered to him.

Now John the Baptist was still baptizing at the Jordan. Jesus went back to the place of his baptism and walked along the river bank toward John and his disciples.

John saw Jesus coming toward him. "Behold the Lamb of God!" he said. "This is he of whom I said: 'After me will come a man who is preferred before me.' "

Two of his disciples heard him say these words. They left John, then, and turned to follow Jesus.

Jesus saw them following. "Whom do you seek?" he asked.

"You, Master," they answered. "Where is your dwelling place?"

"Come, and you shall see," he said.

They went with him to the place where he was staying, and they spent hours listening to him talk. They asked questions, and he answered, and there was no end to what they asked. He talked of peace and love, of repentance and salvation; and the more they heard the more convinced they were that he was the man for whom Israel had been waiting for these many years. He did not look like a King, but he spoke like a Messiah.

One of the two who had left John to follow Jesus was a fisherman named Andrew. He became so carried away by the stirring words of this man from Nazareth that he went out to find his brother Simon.

"We have found the Messiah!" Andrew said. "Come with me; hear him for yourself.

Simon had heard much talk of a Messiah within recent days, for there was a feeling of expectation amongst the Jews. He, like many others, had thought that John might be the long-awaited one. Then John had said that he was not. Again Simon, like so many others, half expected the King of the Jews to appear in kingly regalia and quickly sweep their country free of the Roman rulers. No such man had appeared, and now Simon did not know what to believe or expect.

"Come! We have found the Christ!" his brother Andrew urged him.

"Perhaps," said Simon. He was a strong, rock-hard man of the sea, difficult to convince. But he followed Andrew to meet Jesus.

Jesus saw him coming. No one had told him that this large man was Andrew's brother, yet he knew who Simon was. He knew, too, what manner of man he would prove to be. He looked up and greeted the big man.

"You are Simon, son of Jona," he said to Andrew's brother. "But you shall be called Peter, which means stone. For you shall be my rock of strength."

Simon was astonished that Jesus should have known his name. He, too, sat down and questioned Jesus. As he listened he became more and more convinced that this wise and gentle man was the Christ predicted by the prophets of old. And, like his brother and his friend, he decided that he would follow Jesus.

The next day Jesus started back for his own homeland of Galilee. On the way he found a man called Philip, who came from Bethsaida which was the home town of Andrew and Simon Peter.

"Follow me," said Jesus. And Philip followed him.

As they traveled on, Philip listened to the compelling words of this man who surely must be the promised Messiah. And Philip sought out his friend Nathanael to tell him the good news.

"We have found him!" he said joyfully. "We have found the one of whom Moses and the prophets did write. It is Jesus of Nazareth, the son of Joseph."

Nathaneal was skeptical. And he did not like Nazarenes.

"Can any good thing come out of Nazareth?" he said scornfully.

"Come and see," said Philip.

Jesus saw Nathanael coming to him from a great distance. When the man drew near, Jesus said to him: "Behold, Nathanael! A true Israelite indeed, in whom there is no deceit."

"How do you know me?" asked Nathanael, surprised.

"I saw you under the fig tree," Jesus answered. "Before Philip called you, I saw you there."

Nathanael was even more astonished, for the fig tree under whose shade he had been resting was so far away that no ordinary man could possibly have seen him there.

"Master, you are the Son of God!" he said reverently. "You are the King of Israel!"

"Do you believe that only because I said to you that I saw you under the fig tree?" Jesus asked. "You shall see much greater things than that. You will see heaven open, and the angels of God ascending and descending to the Son of man."

They wondered much at what he said. But whenever they were able to leave their work along the shores of Galilee, the men who had chosen to believe in Jesus left everything behind so that they could follow him.

# The Beginning
of the Mission

＊＊＊＊＊＊＊＊＊＊＊＊＊＊＊＊＊＊＊＊＊＊

A few days after Jesus met his new friends there was a wedding in the town of Cana in Galilee. Jesus, his mother Mary, and his followers were all invited. A great feast followed the marriage ceremony and many of the guests stayed on for several days celebrating with much wine and food.

The wine supply ran dry before the feast was over. Mary was helping to look after the guests, for she was a close friend of the hosts, and she was the first to notice that the wine jars were all empty. She quietly called her son Jesus aside, knowing that her friends would feel disgraced if they failed their guests and knowing, too, that Jesus would be able to help in one way or another.

"There is no more wine," she said to Jesus.

"What would you have me do?" asked Jesus. "My hour is not yet come." For he had not yet begun to show his wonderful powers to the world, nor did he feel that they had been intended for the use of thirsty wedding guests.

But Mary was sure that he would find a way to help. She said to the servants, "Whatever my son tells you, be sure to do it."

Now there were six stone water jars standing there for the ceremonial cleansing rites of the Jews, each of them large enough to hold between twenty and thirty gallons of liquid.

And Jesus told the servants: "Fill the waterpots with water." For he had made up his mind to help his friends at this festive time. A beginning must be made sometime, somehow.

The servants filled the tall jars to the brim.

"Now draw some out," said Jesus, "and take it to the master of the feast." It was the custom for the master of the feast to taste each dish of food and each newly opened jar of wine before the guests were served. The servants did as Jesus told them and took a serving from the water jar to the master steward for approval.

He sipped, he swallowed with pleasure. Both the master of the feast and the servants were surprised: the servants because the water had been turned to wine, and the steward because the wine was so extraordinarily good. Now the steward did not know where this fine wine had come from, for the servants who had filled the waterpots had not told him. When he had sipped to his satisfaction he called the bridegroom, saying:

"Every man sets forth his good wine at the beginning of a feast and serves his poorer wine after his guests have already drunk freely. But you have kept your best wine for the last!"

The feast drew to a successful close, and for most of the guests it had been nothing more than a happy wedding party. Yet it was very much more than that. The turning of the water into wine marked the first time that Jesus had used his special powers to perform what is called a miracle. It was only the beginning of a series of unusual signs that were to make him known throughout the land. But it served, at this time, to show the wonder and glory of Jesus to followers who already wanted to believe in him. When they saw what he had done, they did believe.

After this Jesus went down to Capernaum on the

shore of Galilee with his mother, his brothers, and his followers. They stayed for some days, and then Jesus went up to Jerusalem with his friends to celebrate the passover. They went together to the house of God to worship.

There they saw a sight that shocked Jesus to his very soul. The temple court was like a market place. Live oxen, sheep, and doves were being sold to the worshipers for sacrifices. Pigeons fluttered overhead; cattle lowed in their stalls; buyers and sellers bargained with each other within the walls of God's house. Money changers sat behind their tables clinking coins, ready to change foreign currency and large pieces of local money into the silver half-shekels required as contributions from the temple worshipers to the priests. It was supposed to be a place for prayer and meditation; instead it was a chaos of conflicting sounds and smells, part barnyard and part bank.

Jesus was outraged by this desecration of a holy place, the holiest place in all of Palestine. He looked about him and found several lengths of cord, and from these strands he made a little whip or scourge. In itself it was harmless against the thronging crowd, and indeed it was not meant to be a weapon. But Jesus knew how to drive a herd of cattle or a flock of sheep.

He raised the whip and advanced into the crowd of animals and people. Oxen started to move uneasily toward the temple gate and the sheep began to follow after them. The small whip flicked through the air as Jesus moved about the temple. People turned on him in anger; and then backed away when they saw the look of quiet rage upon his face and the determination of his manner. Money changers, salesmen and customers, oxen and sheep, sightseers in the temple court, fled in disorder before the relentless man with the tiny whip. They did not move quickly enough for Jesus. He overturned the tables of the money changers and spilled their silver on the floor. "Outside!" he commanded, snapping the small whip in the air. "Do your business where you will, but not within the temple." And to the people selling doves he said: "Take these things away! Do not make my Father's house a house of merchandise!" The startled salesmen picked up their goods, pocketed their profits, caught their doves, and swiftly left.

Now many Jews were angry with Jesus for having done these things. It had become their custom to barter thus within the temple court, for it was convenient for worshipers to have the animals for sacrifice, and the money changers with their half-shekels, so very near at hand. They could see nothing wrong with what they had been doing. Besides, this man who had driven them out was a stranger to them. Who was he, they asked each other, that he assumed authority to do such things?

No one seemed able to tell them who he was. They went to Jesus themselves. "What sign will you show to us, to prove you have a right to do such things?" they demanded angrily.

"This sign will I give you," Jesus said. "Destroy this temple, and in three days I will raise it up again."

"Three days!" said the Jews. "It has taken forty-six years to build this temple, and you will raise it in three days!"

Their anger changed to mockery, and they turned away. But Jesus had not been talking about the temple in Jerusalem. He had been talking about the temple of his body, and predicting his own death and resurrection. This was a sign indeed, if the Jews had only thought about it; but they did not think.

While he was at the passover festival in Jerusalem, Jesus began to teach and show other signs that made many people believe he must surely be the Son of God. The Pharisees, however, were not among his believers. Most of them were proud and stiff-necked people who were convinced that only they and the scribes of the priesthood were capable of understanding and interpreting the Laws of God. They refused to admit that either

John or Jesus could have been sent by God to show not only the multitudes, but the Pharisees themselves, the error of their ways. To them, the teachings of Jesus were wrong, and the believers in Jesus had allowed themselves to be misled.

But among the Pharisees was a man named Nicodemus, a rich man and a leader in his community; and he came secretly to Jesus by night to talk to him.

"Master," he said, "we know that you are a teacher who has come from God, for no man could do these miracles that you do unless God were with him." And he told Jesus how strongly he desired to be a true believer and enter the kingdom of God.

"Unless a man is born again," Jesus answered him, "he cannot see the kingdom of God."

"I do not understand," said Nicodemus. "How can a man be born again when he is already old? Can he be a baby for a second time, and be born twice from his mother?"

That was not what Jesus meant. "To be born again is to become as pure as a child," he explained. "It is the spirit, not the body, which must be born anew, for that which is born of the flesh is only flesh; and that which is born of the Spirit, is Spirit. I say unto you that, if a man is not born of water and Spirit, he cannot enter into the kingdom of God. But he that believes and is baptized shall be born again. Then shall the Spirit of God be in his heart, and then shall he be able to enter the kingdom. And I tell you, too, that God so loved the world that he gave his only begotten Son so that whoever believes in him shall not perish, but shall have everlasting life in the kingdom of God."

They talked on into the night and Nicodemus the Pharisee went away with much to think about. It seemed to him that this gentle Jesus must surely be the Son of God, and that his message of love and redemption was much more likely to be the truth than the rigid, ritualistic teachings of the Pharisees and Sadducees.

After these things had happened, Jesus went with his followers into the countryside of Judea. He stayed there with them for some time while they baptized certain newcomers to their ranks, for they had adopted John's practice of purifying by water. Jesus himself did not baptize, but taught among the people who came for baptism.

John was baptizing not far away at a place where there were many waters. A question of purification arose between some of John's disciples and a man of Judea, and this led to a discussion of the baptisms conducted by the followers of Jesus. John's disciples went to their leader and said to him: "Master, the man who was with you across the Jordan, the one to whom you yourself bore witness, behold, that same man is baptizing, and now everyone is going to him."

It was not quite true that Jesus was baptizing, but it was true that people were flocking to hear him teach and be baptized by his loyal followers, thus entering into the brotherhood of those who followed Jesus. John already knew about it, and was far from being jealous. He had known that this must happen.

"A man can receive nothing unless it is given to him from heaven," he answered his disciples. "It is not given to me to have what Jesus has. You yourselves bear me witness that I said, 'I am not the Christ, but he who was sent before him.' He has what I have not, but so it was intended, and I myself rejoice therefore. My happiness is now fulfilled. For he shall grow greater and greater, and I shall grow less and less."

It was true indeed that John's work was nearly done. He still preached against Herod Antipas for marrying Herodias, onetime wife of Herod's brother Philip, and though Herod himself was not greatly troubled by the prophet's words his wife Herodias was steadily stoking the fire of her rage and hatred. Word went out from Galilee to Judea that John must be found at once and seized.

Jesus, in the meanwhile, had left Judea and was

traveling through Samaria on his way back to his own homeland of Galilee. Jews and Samaritans traditionally hated each other, yet Jesus the Jew spoke to the Samaritans as he spoke to everyone, and they listened to him when he told them how to love and worship God their Father. By the time he left Samaria there were many Samaritans who believed that he was the Messiah, the Savior of the world.

And by that time, too, John had been seized and bound. While Jesus journeyed into Galilee, John was lying in prison after once more saying to Herod:

"It is not lawful for you to have your brother's wife!" This statement he had added to a list of Herod's other evils, and it made Herodias boil with rage.

"Kill him!" she had screamed.

But Herod would not have John killed. He knew that John was not only a righteous man but a man with many followers, and he was afraid to put the prophet to death because of what the multitude might do. It was enough, he thought, to keep the man quiet in his prison cell.

As it happened, his wife Herodias did not think it was enough. But she kept her counsel and bided her time.

## *Jesus in Galilee*

✠✠✠✠✠✠✠✠✠✠✠✠✠✠✠✠✠✠✠✠✠✠

Jesus came again to Cana in Galilee where he had made the water into wine. The people of Galilee awaited him with high hopes, for his fame was beginning to spread. They had heard of the miracle of the wine, and the many wonderful signs he had shown while in Jerusalem for the passover, and they looked forward with eagerness to seeing his wonders for themselves.

Now there was a certain nobleman, one of King Herod's officers, who lived in Capernaum. When he heard that Jesus had arrived in Cana he left his home at once and journeyed with all possible haste to meet him and ask for help. The nobleman's small son was dangerously ill, and there was not a doctor in the land who could cure him of his raging fever. The little boy was growing hourly worse, and now it seemed that he would surely die.

The man traveled hard until at last he reached Cana. There he sought out Jesus, finding him by the crowds that always gathered around, and implored the Nazarene to come with him.

"I beg you to come down and heal my son," he said anxiously, "for the boy is at the point of death."

Jesus slowly shook his head. Many people came to him in the hope of seeing some miracle that would prove his powers. Yet he had not come to earth to show that he was a magician; he had come to lead his people into the kingdom of God, and he wanted their belief without first having to show some miraculous sign. If this nobleman was like so many others, he would want to see the miracle before offering his belief. Therefore, Jesus hesitated.

"Except you see signs and wonders done," he said to the nobleman, "you will not believe."

"Sir, I pray you!" the nobleman insisted earnestly. "Come down with me, before my child is dead!"

Jesus searched the nobleman's face, and he saw that this man's need was real.

"Go your way," he said. "Your child will live."

The man believed him. He turned away at once, not questioning, not doubting, and started on his long journey back to Capernaum. He had not even reached the city when his servants came out along the road to meet him. There was great joy on their faces.

"Your son lives! He is well!" they cried out gladly.

"I knew he would be," the nobleman said quietly. "What time was it when he began to get better?"

"It was yesterday at the seventh hour that the fever left him," they answered.

At that same hour, as the father knew, Jesus had said to him: "Your son will live."

Later, when the nobleman had seen his child, he told his household what had happened. From that time onward, not only he but all his family and all the members of his household believed that Jesus had been sent by God.

It was the second miracle that Jesus did in Galilee, and it was even more wonderful than the first. This man, who spoke so gently and with such inspired wisdom, was not only a powerful preacher, a worker of miraculous signs, but a healer as well.

Jesus traveled on through Galilee, talking to people at the wayside and teaching in the synagogues on the sabbath days. He came at last to Nazareth, where he had been brought up, and went into the synagogue on the sabbath day according to his custom. The people of his town had heard much about what he had said and done in other places, and now they wanted to see what he would do in Nazareth. The synagogue was crowded with the curious and devout, and there was silence as he stood up and opened the book written by the prophet Isaiah hundreds of years before. He found the place he sought, and read:

> " 'The Spirit of the Lord is upon me,
>     Because he has anointed me to preach the
>         gospel to the poor;
>     He has sent me to heal the broken-hearted,
>     To preach deliverance to the captives,
>     And recovery of sight to the blind,
>     To set at liberty those that are bruised,
>     And to preach the chosen year of the Lord.' "

He closed the book and gave it back to the attendant, and then sat down to explain the meaning of the passage whose words they already knew so well. They knew that it referred to the Messiah. But they did not know when this Messiah was to come or what he would be like, although they did expect him to be a conquering king. All eyes were fastened on him; all his friends and neighbors waited with quickening interest for what Jesus had to say. They knew he was a healer, they had heard of his wisdom, but they still thought of him as a man very little different from themselves.

His next words astonished them.

He said: "Today has this scripture been fulfilled in your ears."

At first they did not realize what he meant. But then

they stirred and whispered to each other, wondering at his words. For he had said that he was the one of whom the prophet had written, that *he* was the Son of God!

"Is this not Joseph's son?" they asked each other. "Is not his mother called Mary? Who is he that he should say these things?"

They looked at him resentfully. He was a healer and a teacher, yes, and perhaps a prophet; but still he was only their neighbor, only the son of a carpenter, only a man born on earth like all the rest of them. Now he was suggesting that he was the Messiah, the King and Savior of the Jews! Where was all the power and splendor that everyone expected of a divine King?

Jesus knew that they did not believe him, that they would expect him to perform some miraculous feat before their very eyes to prove his words. But that was not the nature of his teaching. Only those who had faith and accepted Jesus could receive his blessings. Even the Roman nobleman had understood that; but the Jews of Nazareth did not.

So Jesus said to them: "You will surely say to me, 'Physician, heal your own. What we have heard you to have done in Capernaum, do also in your own country.' But I say to you, no prophet is accepted in his own country or by his own people. There were many widows in Israel in the days of Elijah, when the heavens were shut for three years and six months so that no rain fell and there was famine in the land. But they did not believe in him; to none of them was he sent by the Lord. No, he was sent to a city of Sidon, to a Phoenician woman who was a widow. She cared for him, believed in him; and God cared for her through Elijah. And there were many lepers in Israel at the time of Elisha the prophet. None of them were cleansed, for they did not believe. But Naaman the Syrian was cured of his leprosy, for he believed and sought Elisha's help. And, like the people of Israel in those days, *you* do not believe!"

All the people in the synagogue were filled with wrath when they heard him say these things. Their admiration turned to sudden hatred and they rose up, shouting with rage. To this sort of teaching, to these words from a fellow Nazarene of all people, they surely would not listen! They laid rough hands on him and thrust him out of the synagogue and out of the city of Nazareth. Then they led him to the top of the craggy hill upon which the city was built so that they might cast him headlong over the side of it. Somehow he escaped them. They did not even notice until they were on the hilltop and ready to throw him down onto the rocks below that he had passed quietly through their midst and gone along his way.

Jesus went back to Capernaum and made his home there among friends. His followers went about their daily work while Jesus taught in the synagogues on sabbath days and preached the gospel of the kingdom of God to the people who lived near the shores of the inland sea of Galilee.

"Repent!" he would say. "The time is fulfilled, and the kingdom of God is at hand. Repent, and believe in the gospel!"

Then word came to him of John the Baptist's imprisonment, and he knew that it was time to make even greater efforts to bring salvation to his people. There were so many still to reach that he could no longer work alone. He had many followers who called themselves disciples because they had elected to believe in his teachings, but Jesus himself had not yet selected those among them who were worthy to spread his word abroad. The time to choose them, however, was drawing very near.

One morning, as he taught beside the sea of Galilee, the people pressing on him from every side to hear his words and to receive his healing touch, he saw two fishing boats drawn up on the shore. The fishermen worked nearby, washing their nets after a long night's work.

Jesus went on teaching, and the crowd grew even greater. Soon it became difficult for him to see any of them but those who pressed against him, and impossible for him to reach the ears and hearts of all. He made his way to one of the nearby boats, which was Simon Peter's, and stepped aboard.

"Put me out a little way from the shore," he asked his friend, and Simon Peter did so. When the boat stopped in the shallow water just offshore Jesus sat down and taught the people from it. When he had finished speaking he turned again to Simon.

"Put me out into the deep water," he said, "and let your nets down for a catch."

Now it was full daylight at the time, and not an hour at which the fishermen of Galilee were used to putting out to sea. Jesus knew as well as any man that the time for fishing was at night.

"Master," Simon answered, "we have toiled all night and have taken nothing." Jesus knew this; he had seen the empty nets they had brought in from the sea. "But," Simon Peter added as he looked at Jesus, "at your word I will let down the nets." He called to his brother Andrew to bring the nets, which were still drying in the sun, and the two brothers rowed out into deeper waters as Jesus had instructed them.

When they were some distance out they stopped and let down the nets. And in a matter of minutes the nets were filled with darting, glittering fish, a catch such as Simon had never seen in all his years of fishing. There seemed no end to the shining shapes that flashed around the boat. Simon and Andrew began to haul in with all their strength. But so great was the shoal and so heavy was the precious catch that the thick strands of their nets began to part. They shouted for their partners John and James, who were working in the other boat beached upon the shore, for they needed help with this tremendous haul. The two men came out at once and lent their willing hands to pulling in the sagging, tearing nets, and when at last they had brought the catch aboard both boats were filled so full that they began to sink.

When Simon Peter saw what was happening he fell down at Jesus' feet in the overloaded boat and cried out: "Leave me, O Lord, for I am a sinful man!" It had been almost too much for him; he was astonished at the great haul of fishes they had taken, and so were all the other men who had fished all night and caught not one.

"Do not be afraid," said Jesus. "From now on, you will catch men instead of fish."

They landed their boats safely and unloaded their huge catch.

And the next day when Jesus walked by the sea of Galilee and saw Simon Peter and his brother Andrew casting their nets into the sea, he said to them: "Come, follow me, and I will make you fishers of men."

They left their nets at once and followed him.

When they had gone a little further along the shore Jesus saw James and John in their boat with their father Zebedee, mending their nets. And Jesus called to James and John. "Come, follow me," he said.

And at once the brothers left their boat with their father Zebedee and his servants, and they followed Jesus.

Thus did Jesus choose the first four of his disciples. With them he went all about the land of Galilee, teaching in the synagogues and preaching the gospel of God's kingdom.

# The Miracles
## of Jesus

✠✠✠✠✠✠✠✠✠✠✠✠✠✠✠✠✠✠✠✠✠

Jesus and his four disciples went together to Capernaum, and there Jesus entered into the synagogue and taught the people on the sabbath day. They were astonished at his teachings, his words were full of power and he spoke as one who had authority from God, and not as the scribes, who did little more than repeat what they had read.

Now there was in the synagogue a man who was possessed by an unclean spirit, a demon that made him cry out in a loud voice:

"Let us alone! What have we to do with you, Jesus of Nazareth? Have you come to destroy us? I know who you are—the Holy One of God!"

Jesus rebuked the demon in the man. "Be silent; hold your peace," he said. "Come out of him."

The spirit made the man shake violently and fall down upon the floor. There was a loud cry, and then silence. The man got up, unhurt in his body and peaceful in his mind. The unclean spirit had left him.

The people who saw this were understandably amazed. They talked among themselves. "What thing is this?" they asked each other. "What new teaching can this be? See with what authority and power he gives commands to unclean spirits, and they do obey him!"

And immediately the fame of Jesus spread throughout all the region round about.

When Jesus left the synagogue that day he went into the house of Simon and Andrew, together with the brothers James and John. And Simon found that his wife's mother was lying ill, burning with a fever. Jesus went in at once to see her. He stood beside her bed, took her by the hand, and gently raised her up. Immediately the fever left her, and she arose from her bed. At once she went about her household in good spirits and good health, and within minutes she was preparing a meal for Simon Peter and his guests.

That evening, as the sun was setting on the sabbath day, the people of the neighborhood brought to Jesus all the sick folk among their friends and families and all those who were possessed by demonic spirits. It seemed as though the whole town had gathered at the door of Simon Peter's house: the diseased, the lame, the blind, and the troubled in spirit. Jesus laid his hands on every one of them, and healed all who were sick.

It was late before the throng of people left the house of Simon, and Jesus was at last able to lie down and sleep. And yet it was very early in the morning when he rose and walked alone into the desert until he found a solitary place where he could stop and pray. It was peaceful for a time, but even here the people sought him out and eventually found him. Simon and his companions reached Jesus first.

"Everyone is seeking you," they said to him. "They want you to stay with them, but they are afraid that you will leave this place."

"They are right," said Jesus. "I must leave here. Come with me; let us go into the next towns so that I may preach in them as well, for I have been sent to proclaim the good tidings of the kingdom of God in other cities, too."

They left Capernaum then, and went together

throughout all Galilee. Jesus preached in synagogues and cast out many demons that were troubling people's souls; and the report of him went out as far as Syria. He healed the epileptic and the palsied, the diseased and the tormented; and great multitudes followed him from Galilee and Decapolis and Jerusalem and Judea and from beyond the Jordan.

While he was in a certain town a leper came to him and knelt before him, worshiping. No man would touch a leper, and the sick man knew it, for he had spent his life seeing people turn away when he came near. Yet he knelt at Jesus' feet and begged for help, and Jesus did not turn away.

"If you will," the leper said, "you can make me clean."

And Jesus, moved with compassion, stretched forth his hand and touched him. "I will," he said. "Be healed."

As soon as he had spoken, the leprosy left the man and he was clean.

Then Jesus said to him: "See that you say nothing of this to any man. Go your way, show yourself to the priest, and make such offerings for your cleansing as Moses commanded so that the priest will pronounce you clean of leprosy. But do not speak of me to anyone."

The leper gave his thanks and went away. But instead of obeying Jesus' request to be silent about his cure he went around talking about the wonderful thing that had happened to him, spreading his news abroad so widely that great multitudes flocked to the town to listen to Jesus and be healed of their infirmities. So huge were the crowds that Jesus could no longer enter the city openly. Instead, he stayed outside in a desert place, hoping to use it as a base from which he could move about freely. But even there, people came to him from every quarter so that it was almost impossible for him to leave the place and go about his mission.

Several days later he managed to get back to Capernaum. It was not long before the people of the city found out that he was at home (for since his rejection at Nazareth he had made his home in Capernaum), and they immediately gathered at his house to hear his words and receive his healing touch. The friendly and the curious, the needy and the sick, all crowded in and filled the house. Even Pharisees, and scribes or doctors of the law, had come from every town of Galilee and Judea to listen to this man. In a very short time the place was so full that there was not an inch of space to spare, not even at the open door. And Jesus preached the word of God to them in that overcrowded room.

Now there was a man who was so ill and crippled with the palsy that he could not drag himself about in search of Jesus nor go up to him when he had found him. And when he did discover through friends where Jesus was, it seemed that there was no way to force the crowds to part and let him into the house. But he had four friends who were as sure as he that Jesus would be able to cure him, and they were determined that he should be healed. They carried him on his pallet to the house where Jesus was.

By now even the street outside the house was so packed with people that they almost despaired. The four friends looked about to find some other means of bringing the palsied man to Jesus, and at last they thought of a way. Carrying the sick man on the cot with the utmost care, they climbed onto the housetop and broke open a section of the roof. Then, slowly and carefully, they lowered their friend through the tiling and set him down, bed and all, in the midst of the throng pressing around Jesus.

Jesus looked down at the man, and up at the four friends on the roof. And seeing their faith, he said to the one who was sick of the palsy:

"Son, be of good cheer. Your sins are forgiven."

The sick man's heart was lightened. But certain of the scribes and Pharisees who were sitting there were thinking harsh things within themselves. In their hearts they questioned Jesus' right to say such words to any man. To them, those words were blasphemy. "Who is he, that he should speak such blasphemies?" they asked themselves. "Why does he say these things? Who can forgive sins but God alone?" Thus did they reason in their hearts, and they doubted Jesus, for they did not want to believe that Jesus had been sent by God and that he, too, had the power of forgiveness. No, they would rather believe that he was an ordinary man speaking impiously of God.

Jesus could see what they were thinking. He answered their unspoken words at once. "Why do you think evil of me in your hearts?" he asked. "And what is it that you are reasoning within yourselves—whether it is easier to say to the man sick with the palsy, 'Your sins are forgiven,' or, 'Arise, take up your bed and walk'? Yes, it is easy indeed to pretend power, to talk rather than do. But do you think that forgiveness cannot be demonstrated? I will show you now that the Son of man does have authority on earth to forgive sins."

He turned to the palsied man, still lying ill and paralyzed on his pallet in the midst of the gaping crowd, and he said: "I say to you: Arise, take up your bed and go to your own house."

Immediately the man rose, took up his bed, and pushed his way through the crowd. He headed for his own house, praising God and talking excitedly to his four loyal friends, and all who saw him were amazed. They marveled, they feared, they glorified the God of Jesus; and they said: "We have seen strange things today."

Stranger things were yet to come.

Jesus went forth again by the seaside. The multitude followed him as usual, and he taught them as he walked. One day as he passed by, he saw a publican named Levi, also known as Matthew, sitting at the toll house where the tax money was collected. Matthew was hated by the Jews because he was a tax collector for the Romans. It did not occur to them that he might not be a sinner, for they had suffered from the dishonesty and greed of tax collectors through many years of Roman rule.

And to this man Matthew, hated tax collector, Jesus spoke two words:

"Follow me."

Matthew arose and followed him.

Some time afterward Matthew made a feast for Jesus in his house, to which he invited a great company of fellow publicans and other people whom the self-righteous Pharisees regarded as unfit companions for all right-thinking Jews. When the Pharisees saw that Jesus and his disciples sat at meat with Matthew and the others, they murmured against Jesus and his friends.

"Why do you and your Master sit down with tax collectors and sinners?" they asked the disciples.

When Jesus heard the murmurings of the Pharisees he went to them and said: "Those who are well have no need of a physician, only those who are sick. And those who are without sin have no need of me. I did not come to call the righteous, but sinners to repentance."

Matthew, the tax collector, did not think he was so righteous that he had no need to repent. He knew that he had sinned, and he was humble. But the Pharisees could see no flaws in themselves, and they were proud. Thus they could not see that their need to repent was even greater than that of the self-admitted sinner Matthew.

For some time they were satisfied with Jesus' reply. Then they thought of something else to complain about. They went to Jesus and said: "Why do the disciples of John fast often and make prayers, and also the disciples of the Pharisees, while your disciples do not fast and seem always to be eating and drinking?"

"Can you expect the wedding guests to fast and mourn while the bridegroom is with them?" Jesus asked in return. "As long as they have the bridegroom with them, they cannot and should not fast. But the day will come when the bridegroom shall be taken away from them, and then will they fast."

The Pharisees did not know quite what to make of this, and they went away to think of further cause for complaint against Jesus and his followers. But what Jesus had meant was that he himself would one day be taken from his disciples, and then indeed would they pray and fast.

It was not altogether true that the disciples of Jesus were always eating and drinking, in spite of what the Pharisees had said, for they were simple men of scanty means and in their travels with Jesus through the countryside they often went hungry. Tax collectors did not often invite them home to dine, nor were there inns in the desert places where they often taught.

On a certain day it happened that their way led through some grainfields. The disciples had not eaten for some time. So they began, as they went through the tall grain, to pluck the ripe ears, rub off the chaff, and eat. The watching Pharisees, always with them, again had comments to offer.

"Behold!" they said to Jesus. "Why do your followers do on the sabbath day that which is not lawful to do?" For they regarded this simple action of the disciples as a crime, that of working on the sabbath day.

To Jesus, what the Pharisees had done to the day of rest was little short of ridiculous. Under their teachings the sabbath had become so enmeshed in a web of law and ritual that it was a day of torment rather than rest. But he answered patiently and with quiet logic.

"Have you never read in the scriptures what David did when he had need, and was hungry, as were those who were with him? How he went into the house of God in the days of Abiathar the high priest, and ate the sacred bread which is only lawful for the priests to eat, and also gave it to those who were with him? Or do you not realize that even the priests in the temple work on the sabbath, offering sacrifices in the morning and the evening? Yet you hold them guiltless, even though they

work! And this I say to you: something greater than the
temple is here, and something greater than the sabbath.
The Lord desires mercy, and not sacrifice. If you would
only understand! The sabbath was made for man, and
not man for the sabbath. And the Son of man is Lord
even of the sabbath."

That, indeed, was something that they did not understand. As the Lord on earth, Jesus was Lord of the
sabbath as well as everything else. But this was beyond
their understanding and always would be. To them,
Jesus of Nazareth was only a man.

Jesus and his disciples made their way back to the
city and went again into the synagogue. There was a
man there who had a withered hand. The scribes and
the Pharisees watched eagerly to see whether Jesus
would heal the man on the sabbath day, so that they
might once again accuse him.

And again Jesus knew their thoughts. He said to the
man with the withered hand: "Rise up; stand forth in
their midst." The man stood up and faced Jesus before
all the silent watchers.

According to the Pharisees, even healing was work,
and not the sort of work that Jesus could justify by
quoting from the scriptures or pointing to the priests.
And so they waited to see what Jesus would do on this
sabbath day with the man whose hand was withered.

"I will ask you one thing," Jesus said to them. "Is it
lawful to do good on the sabbath days, or to do evil? Is
it good to save life, or to kill?"

They were silent, waiting. They could not answer
him.

Jesus went on: "What man is there among you, that
shall have one sheep which falls into a pit on the
sabbath day, who would not lift it out? And of how
much more value is a man than a sheep! Therefore, it is
lawful to do good on the sabbath days. Stretch out your
hand!"

Jesus looked around the hall, his heart grieving at the
hardness of the Pharisees' hearts. But the man, believ-

ing, stretched out his hand. And in that moment it was restored to health and was as whole as the hand that had not been withered.

The Pharisees were filled with fury. They left the synagogue together to take counsel with each other, and with certain of the lords of Herod's court, as to how they might curb this dangerous lawbreaker. The best idea seemed to be to destroy him. But that seemed a little harsh. As for Jesus, he left the city before they had made up their minds, and withdrew with his disciples to the shores of Galilee.

Some time after these events there was a feast of the Jews, and Jesus went up to Jerusalem to celebrate it. Now there was at this time in Jerusalem, as in the days of old, a pool named Bethesda near the Sheep Gate. Around it, as Jesus saw, there lay a multitude of sick folk: blind, lame, diseased, and withered of limb; and all were waiting for the moving of the water. It was said among them that an angel of the Lord went down into the pool at certain times and stirred the waters, and that the first one who stepped into the waters after they had been troubled would be cured of whatever disease he had. So they waited, each one hoping and praying that he would be the first to move at the stirring of the waters by the angel.

There were some among them who could barely move, so that their chances of reaching the pool before the others were very slight. Thus there was a certain man lying beside the pool who had been ill for thirty-eight years. Each year he struggled to the pool to see the moving of the waters, and each year he failed to reach the water in time. There were always others before him.

When Jesus saw him lying there and knew that he had been in that condition for many years, he approached the man and said: "Do you wish to be made well?"

The sick man answered him: "Sir, I do, but I have no one to help me into the pool when the waters are stirred. Always, while I am on my way, another steps down into the pool before me."

"Rise, take up your bed and walk," Jesus said to him. And even as he spoke, the man was cured. He arose, took up his bed and walked away with gratitude in his heart.

Now it was the sabbath on that day, and those who saw him carrying his pallet stopped him and said: "It is the sabbath. It is not lawful for you to be carrying your bed."

The cured man, well and happy for the first time in thirty-eight years, looked at them and said: "He that made me whole again said to me, 'Take up your bed and walk.' And I did so."

The scribes and Pharisees among the Jews soon found out who had told the man to do this thing, and their outrage knew no bounds. Again, Jesus had healed upon the sabbath day, and this time he had even told a man to carry his own bed—to *work* upon the day proclaimed by God as the day of rest!

They taxed Jesus with this dreadful thing that he had done. He calmly answered, "My Father is still working, even on the sabbath, and I am working, too."

From that day on the Pharisees began to persecute Jesus without mercy. He had not only broken their Law by doing these things upon the sabbath day; but he had also claimed that God was his own Father, making himself equal with God.

They resolved, therefore, to kill him when they could find their chance.

# The Sermon
# on the Mount

✸✸✸✸✸✸✸✸✸✸✸✸✸✸✸✸✸✸✸✸✸✸✸

There were those who followed the letter of the Law, and those who followed the spirit of it as expressed by Jesus.

When Jesus went again to the shores of Galilee, people flocked after him from Jerusalem and all the land of Judea; they came to him from the countryside and towns of Galilee, and from beyond the river Jordan. They heard of him in Tyre, and in Sidon, and in Syria, and they came to see him with their sick and their diseased and all those who were possessed by devils that tormented their souls.

Jesus cured them in their dozens and their scores and in their hundreds. He healed the palsied and the epileptic; he drove off pain and demons and even death itself. It became impossible for him to reach all those who came to him. A time came when he had to ask his disciples to have a boat always waiting for him just offshore so that he could preach from there in case the crowd pressed so heavily upon him that he could not teach or heal. By now his fame was very great, and he had healed so many people that countless numbers came to crowd upon him so that he might touch and cure them.

At last it became obvious that he could not do his work without others to help him, not only with his preaching but his healing. Many men had followed him and were following him still, men who called themselves disciples because they believed in him and loved him, but of them all he had only chosen four to do his work. He knew, now, that he would have to make a further choice. One night, therefore, he went alone up into a mountain to pray; and he passed the entire night in prayer to God his Father.

When it was day he called all of his disciples to him and named the twelve whom he had chosen to be his apostles. These men were to be with him when they could help by being near at hand, and to be sent out at other times to preach in the many places he would not be able to reach if he worked alone. When they came to him he gave to them the power to heal all manner of sickness and disease, and the authority to cast out unclean spirits or demons.

Now the names of the apostles he chose are these: Simon, to whom he had given the name of Peter; Andrew, Simon Peter's brother; James and John, the sons of Zebedee; Philip, and his friend Bartholomew who was also called Nathanael; Thomas; and Matthew, who had been a publican; another James, the son of Alphaeus; another Simon, who was a Canaanite; Judas, also called Thaddaeus, who was the brother of the second James; and Judas Iscariot, who became a traitor.

When Jesus came down the mountain with the chosen twelve he once again saw crowds of people waiting for him. Goodness flowed out of him as the people pressed around and touched him, and he healed all those who were diseased and troubled with unclean spirits. But, seeing the great multitude and knowing that he would see many more like it in the months to come, he decided that he would wait no longer to teach his disciples all he could. He went up into the mountain again with his chosen twelve. There he seated himself. He began to speak, and even as he spoke the crowds came up to listen. But they did not disturb him as he taught the twelve.

"Know this," he said, "and remember always:

"Blessed are the poor in spirit, those who feel their spiritual need, for the kingdom of heaven belongs to them.

"Blessed are those who mourn, for they shall be comforted.

"Blessed are the humble, for they shall inherit the earth.

"Blessed are those who hunger and thirst for righteousness, for they shall be filled.

"Blessed are the merciful, for they shall obtain mercy.

"Blessed are the pure in heart, for they shall see God.

"Blessed are the peacemakers, for they shall be called the children of God.

"Blessed are those who are persecuted because of their righteousness, for theirs is the kingdom of heaven.

"Blessed are you when men shall abuse you, and persecute you, and say all manner of evil against you falsely, for my sake;

"Rejoice, and be exceedingly glad, for great is your reward in heaven; for so persecuted were the prophets who were before you."

For once the great crowd listened in absolute silence as Jesus went on speaking to his twelve disciples and explaining to them what manner of men he wanted them to be, for their own sakes and his.

"You are the salt of the earth," he said. "But if the salt has lost its flavor, how can it be made salty again?

It is then fit for nothing but to be thrown away and trodden underfoot.

"You are the light of the world. A city that is built upon a hill cannot be hidden. Men do not light a candle and then hide it; they put it on a candlestick so that it gives light to everyone in the house. Therefore let your light so shine before men that they may see your good works, and glorify your Father who is in heaven.

"Do not think that I have come to destroy the law or the prophets; I have not come to destroy, but to fulfill. For whoever shall break the least of the commandments and teaches other men to do so, shall be called least in the kingdom of heaven. But whoever shall do them and teach them shall be called great in the kingdom of heaven. I say to you that unless your uprightness exceeds that of the scribes and the Pharisees, you will never enter the kingdom of heaven.

"You have heard that it was said to men in days of old that he who was harmed should exact equal harm in return. 'An eye for an eye, and a tooth for a tooth'; so it was said. But these are not the days of old. I say to you now, do not resist injury, and do not injure in return. If anyone strikes you on your right cheek, turn the other to him also. And if anyone wants to sue you in a court of law and take away your coat, give him your cloak as well. And if anyone compels you to go one mile, go two miles with him. Give to him that asks your help; and if anyone wishes to borrow from you, do not turn away. As you would have men treat you, so should you treat them.

"You have heard that it was said: 'You shall love your neighbor, and hate your enemy.' But I say to you: Love your enemies, and pray for those who persecute you. Then shall you truly be sons of your Father who is in heaven, for he makes his sun rise on the evil as well as the good, and he sends rain to the just and the unjust alike, and he is kind to the unthankful and the evil even as he is kind to the grateful and upright. Be you therefore merciful, even as your Father is merciful.

"For if you only love those who love you, why should you expect reward? Do not even the tax collectors do the same? And if you do good only to those who do good to you, why expect a reward? Even sinners do the same. And if you lend to those from whom you hope to receive, why think that you deserve thanks? Even the sinners lend to sinners, to receive as much again.

"I say to you, it is your enemies that you should love! Bless those who curse you; do good to those who hate you; pray for those who use you badly; and lend to those who need, hoping for nothing in return. Then shall your reward be great!

"Be therefore perfect, as your heavenly Father is perfect.

"And take care that you do not do your good deeds in public in order to be seen by others. If you do, you will get no reward from your Father in heaven. When, therefore, you give to charity, do not blow a trumpet before you as do the hypocrites in the synagogues and in the streets, so that they may be seen and praised. I say to you, the praise of man is all they will get! Instead, when you give alms, do not let your own left hand know what your right hand is doing, so that your charity may be secret. Your Father who sees what you do in secret will reward you openly.

"And when you fast, do not—as the hypocrites do—put on a gloomy look, for they disfigure their faces and make themselves look sad so that all men shall know that they are fasting. That, I say to you, is all the reward they will get. But you, when you fast, anoint your head with perfumes and wash your face, so that no one may know that you are fasting except your Father who is unseen. And your Father, who sees that which is done in secret, will reward you openly.

"And when you pray, do not be like the hypocrites, who love to pray standing in the synagogues and on the corners of the streets so that they may be seen at prayer. I say to you, the praise of men shall be their only reward. But you, when you pray, go into a quiet room, and when you have shut the door, pray to your Father who is unseen. And your Father who sees what you do in secret will reward you openly.

"And in praying, do not use idle repetitions and many empty phrases such as others do, for they imagine they shall be heard if they use many words. Do not be like them, for your Father knows what you have need of before you ask him. Pray, therefore, in this manner:

> "Our Father, which art in heaven,
> Hallowed be thy name.
> Thy kingdom come;
> Thy will be done
> On earth, as it is in heaven.
> Give us this day our daily bread,
> And forgive us our debts,
> As we forgive our debtors.
> And lead us not into temptation,
> But deliver us from evil:
> For thine is the kingdom,
> And the power,
> And the glory,
> For ever! Amen."

There was silence in the multitude. But they wondered at many of the things he said.

"If you forgive others when they do wrong," Jesus went on, "your heavenly Father will forgive you, too. But if you do not forgive others for their wrongs, neither will your Father forgive you for yours."

"And do not store up earthly treasures for yourselves, instead of the riches of the spirit. Rather seek out the kingdom of God, and all other things you need shall be given to you. I say to you, do not concern yourselves about the things of your daily life: what you shall eat, what you shall drink, what you shall wear. Is not life something more than food, and the body of more worth than clothes? Behold the birds of the air!

They do not sow, neither do they reap, nor gather their food into barns. Yet your heavenly Father feeds them. And are you not of much more value than they?

"Which of you, by worrying about these things, can add one inch to his height or one minute to his life? And why should you be anxious concerning clothing? Consider the lilies of the field, how they grow; they toil not, neither do they spin. Yet even Solomon, in all his glory, was not arrayed like one of these. And if God so clothes the wild grass of the field, which grows today and is cast into the furnace tomorrow, shall he not more surely clothe you, O ye of little faith?

"Therefore do not be anxious, saying: 'What shall we eat?' or 'What shall we drink?' or 'How shall we be clothed?' For your heavenly Father knows that you have need of all these things. Seek first the kingdom of God, and his righteousness, and all these things will be freely given you. Be not therefore anxious for the morrow, for the morrow will be anxious for itself. The evils of today are enough for the day.

"Ask, and it shall be given you. Seek, and you shall find. Knock, and the door will open to you. For he who asks of God shall receive; he who searches shall find; and to him who knocks the door shall be opened. And, as you would have other men do to you, do you also to them likewise.

"Each tree is known by its own fruit. No good tree brings forth bad fruit; no bad tree brings forth good fruit. Therefore, by the fruits of men, you shall know them."

Jesus said all these things and many more upon the Mount that day. And at last he said:

"Not everyone who says to me, 'Lord! Lord!' shall enter into the kingdom of heaven, but only those who listen to my words and do the will of my Father in heaven. I say to you now, you must be ready for the day when you are called to God. I will show you what the man is like who comes to me, hears my words, and acts according to them: He is like a man who, in building his house, dug down deep and laid the foundation upon a rock. When the rain fell, the floods came, and the storm winds blew and beat upon that house, it stood firm and did not fall because it was founded upon the rock. But everyone who hears these words of mine and does not act upon them shall be like a foolish man who built his house upon the sand. When the rain fell, the floods came, and the storm winds beat against it, the house upon the sand broke into pieces. Great was the fall thereof!

"But if you build your lives according to my words, you will be building on a rock foundation."

When Jesus had finished speaking the people were astonished at his words. For he taught them as one who had authority, and not as the scribes who quoted the old laws to them and never once said such strange things as: "Love your enemies. Bless those who curse you. Do good to those who hate you. Turn the other cheek."

These ideas were new to them. They did not sound at all like the preachings of the Pharisees. But to the thoughtful ones in the multitude the sayings of Jesus truly sounded as though they were the words of a merciful and loving God.

# Jesus
# and John the Baptist

�֎✥✥✥✥✥✥✥✥✥✥✥✥✥✥✥✥✥✥✥✥✥

After he had ended all his sayings on the mountain, Jesus entered into the city of Capernaum. Now a certain centurion was there, a Roman captain over a hundred soldiers, who had a faithful bondservant of whom he was exceedingly fond. He was little more than a youth, this servant, but he lay ill with palsy to the point of death.

When the centurion heard of Jesus and discovered that he was in Capernaum even now he went to some of the elders of the Jews and asked them for their help. He was hesitant to approach the healer himself, for he was a humble man even though a captain of men.

"My servant lies at home, sick of the palsy and grievously tormented," the centurion told the elders. "I beg you, go to the healer Jesus and beseech him to come and save my servant."

The elders went at once to seek out Jesus, and earnestly requested him to go with them and heal the centurion's young servant. "This Roman is a worthy man," they said. "He is deserving of help, for he loves our nation and has himself built us our synagogue."

Jesus turned and went with them. When he was not

very far from the house, the centurion sent friends out to him with a message. "Lord, do not trouble yourself," his message said, "for I am not worthy that you should enter under my roof. Neither did I think myself worthy to come to you. But only say the word, and my servant shall be healed."

When Jesus heard these words he marveled greatly. He turned to those who had followed him to the house and said, "I say to you, I have not found such faith in all of Israel—no, not among the Jews—as this Roman has shown!" And to the centurion's friends he said, "Go your way. As the man has believed, so shall it be done."

And when those who had been sent to speak to Jesus went back into the house, they found the servant cured of his sickness.

On the day after that, Jesus went into another city called Nain. Many of his disciples and other people followed him. When he came near to the gate of the city, Jesus and his disciples saw a funeral procession winding slowly toward them, and in the midst of it was the dead man being carried from the city in his coffin. The man was young, too young to have to die, and he was the only son of his mother who was a widow. The woman wept and mourned, and there were many people of the city with her as she walked along in sorrow.

The two groups met at the gate of Nain, the mourners with the bier and Jesus with his followers. Jesus looked at the woman. Her tears were bitter, for all she loved had been taken from her, and she mourned with all the sorrow of her heart. When Jesus saw her grief he felt a deep compassion for her. "Do not weep," he said to her. Jesus went up and touched the bier. The bearers stopped and stood still with their burden while this gentle stranger looked down at the dead face.

"Young man, I say to you, arise!" he said.

And the young man who had been dead sat up and began to speak. The widow woman ran to her son with tears upon her cheeks that now were tears of joy, for

Jesus had given her back her only child. The cries of sorrow from those in the procession turned to cries of amazement and fear. Those who had seen what Jesus had done praised God and glorified him, saying, "A great prophet has appeared among us! God has visited his people."

And this rumor about Jesus spread throughout all the region round about, which was southern Galilee, and throughout all Judea.

Jesus continued with his work in that part of Galilee, preaching his message of salvation and healing the sick, until word of his wonders reached the disciples of John. They went to him and told him all these things. Now John was still in Herod's prison, but the king on occasion permitted him to be visited by his friends. When the Baptist heard in prison about the works of Jesus he could not keep from thinking about his own plight. If it was indeed true that Jesus could do the marvelous things that were rumored of him, why did he not use his powers to free John? And although Jesus had referred to himself as the Son of man and the Son of God, he had never said directly that he was the Christ. Was he, or was he not, the long-awaited Messiah and King of the Jews?

Alone in prison, John's faith wavered. He had been the first to acknowledge Jesus as the Anointed One. But now he felt within himself a small doubt.

John thought long about these things. And at last he sent for two of his disciples. "Go to Jesus," he said to them. "Ask him this: 'Are you he that is promised, or do we look for another?' "

They went at once to Jesus with the questions John had instructed them to ask. Jesus understood at once that John had need of reassurance, yet he could not announce himself directly as the Messiah, for then not only the priests and Pharisees but Herod himself would have reason to condemn him. And for the same reason, he could not use his powers to free John. He still had work to do and little enough time in which to do it.

Nevertheless, he must send a message to John that would convince him that the Messiah had indeed come.

While John's disciples watched, Jesus cured many people of their illnesses, and many of evil spirits; and to many that were blind he gave their sight. John's disciples saw lepers becoming clean, and saw cripples walk away, and they heard the gentle words that Jesus spoke. Evenutally Jesus turned again to them.

"Go and tell John what you have seen and heard," he said. "Tell him how the blind receive their sight, how the lame walk and the lepers are cleansed, how the deaf hear and the dead are raised; and how the poor are being preached the good tidings of the kingdom of God."

Jesus knew that John would understand from these things that he truly was the Messiah, for they both knew the words of Isaiah concerning the One who was to come:

> "Say to them that are of a fearful heart:
> Be strong, fear not;
> Behold, your God will come with vengeance,
> God himself with a just reward;
> He will come and save you.
> Then the eyes of the blind shall be opened,
> And the ears of the deaf shall be unstopped.
> Then shall the lame man leap as a hart,
> And the tongue of the dumb sing;
> For in the wilderness shall waters break out,
> And streams in the desert."

By these words would John be answered. Jesus sorrowed for his plight, but there was nothing he could do except send him that message. And Jesus knew that John had more need for reassurance about the Messiah than he had desire to be helped by miracles himself. "Say this also to him," Jesus said to John's disciples. "Say: 'Blessed is he who never doubts me.' "

The two men went back to John with a report of

Jesus' works among the people and the things that he had said.

When they had gone, Jesus began to speak to the crowds about the prophet John. "When you went out into the wilderness to hear the words of John," he began, "what did you go to see? A reed swaying in the wind? No, that was not what you wanted to see. And did you think you would see a man clothed in soft raiment? No, for those who are luxuriously dressed live in the houses of kings. Then what did you go out to see? A prophet? Yes! You saw a prophet, and much more than a prophet. This is the man of whom it is written:

"Behold, I send my messenger before your face,
Who shall prepare the way before you!"

"John is that man, and I say to you that among those born of women, there is not a greater prophet than John the Baptist. Yet, great though John is, he who is least in the kingdom of heaven is greater than he. Those who listened and were baptized were absolved of sin in the eyes of God. But the Pharisees and the scribes, being not baptized, rejected for themselves the counsel of God. Therefore I say, whoever has ears to hear, let him hear. Believe, and act accordingly."

John the Baptist heard the news of Jesus' healing works, and also of the tribute paid to him by the man he now believed unquestioningly to be the Messiah. And this message was the last one brought to him about the powers and sayings of Jesus.

King Herod's wife, Herodias, still nursed her hatred for the imprisoned prophet. She would have had him killed the moment he was seized, but Herod had denied her every plea. For Herod feared John, knowing that he was a just and holy man, and he had refused to harm him. Indeed, he spoke kindly to the prophet and listened to his words. In the course of John's imprisonment he had spoken often to him, learning much; and of late he had even showed some signs of changing his evil ways.

But Herodias was still looking for revenge. Now she saw her chance through her daughter, a dancer of much grace and skill, who had been born to her when she had been Philip's wife. For Herod, on his birthday, gave a banquet for his courtiers, high captains, and the leading men of Galilee, and this lovely daughter came in at her mother's request and danced before the king and his illustrious guests. All were delighted by her sinuous dance. When it was over the king, mellowed with wine, called to the girl and said: "Ask of me what you will, and I will give it to you. You have my oath upon it! Whatever you ask I will give, up to half my kingdom."

The girl had need of nothing for herself, but she knew her mother had a request to make. Therefore she left the banquet room and went to see her mother, who had chosen to wait discreetly in the background.

"What shall I ask for?" the girl said to her waiting mother.

The evil woman made no attempt to conceal her eagerness.

"The head of John the Baptist!" she replied triumphantly.

The girl went back to Herod. "My wish is that you will forthwith give me the head of John the Baptist on a platter!"

Herod was shocked into sudden sobriety. He had made a foolish oath before all the people of the crowded banquet hall, and the consequences of it were upon him. His heart was sorely troubled and he was exceedingly sorry for the rash promise he had made, for he still had no wish to kill the earnest Baptist from whom he had begun to learn so much. But because of his oath, and the guests who sat there watching him and waiting for his answer, he knew that he could not refuse her. He hesitated only briefly. Then he sent a guard with a message for his executioner: "Bring the head of John the Baptist into the banquet hall at once!"

The executioner went down into the dungeon and performed his grisly task. When he had done so, he brought John's head into the great hall upon a serving platter and gave it to the girl. She did not want it; she gave it to her mother. Her mother took it gladly, smiling exultantly at the pathetic sight. That tongue would never again speak harsh words against Herodias.

When John's disciples heard the dreadful news they came to the prison and removed the body so that they might give it the respectful burial John deserved. Then they went to Jesus and told him what had happened.

He sorrowed deeply for his cousin the prophet, he who had gone before to prepare the way. But with the death of John, Jesus' work had become even more urgent. He called together his twelve apostles to teach them all he could, and he urged them to redouble their efforts. He himself called on all his time and energy to travel about preaching and healing before time ran out altogether.

Jesus knew that his danger was increasing daily. It would not be long before Herod began to express an interest in him, and not a friendly interest; and at the same time the scribes and Pharisees were becoming more and more outraged by the doctrine that he preached. Already they had held meetings with the Herodians as to how they might silence what they thought of as his "blasphemy" and "heresy." Yet he continued working even harder than before and speaking to people with growing urgency.

He went about through cities and villages, preaching and bringing to his hearers the good tidings of the kingdom of God. With him went the twelve, and certain women, too, who had been healed of evil spirits and infirmities: Mary of Magdala, who was called Mary Magdalene, from whom he had cast out seven devils;

Joanna, the wife of Herod's steward; and a woman named Susanna, and many others, who helped to look after the needs of Jesus and his disciples. Together they journed through Galilee to spread the gospel message.

# Parables
# and Miracles in Galilee

✳✳✳✳✳✳✳✳✳✳✳✳✳✳✳✳✳✳✳✳✳✳✳

One day Jesus went out to teach again upon the shores of Galilee. At first he sat down at the seaside to talk to those who gathered, but as before the crowd pressing against him became so vast that it was difficult for him to talk to all and be heard. And again he got into a boat and sat down in it to teach the people while they listened from the shore.

This time he did not talk directly of the kingdom of God and man's need for repentance. Instead, he chose to teach in parables, short stories to illustrate the meaning of his lessons. Yet all the stories he told that day concerned the kingdom of heaven.

"Behold!" he began. "There was a farmer who went into his field to sow seeds of grain. And as he walked back and forth scattering the grain, some of the seed fell by the wayside, and the birds of the air flew down and ate it up. And some of the seed fell on rocky ground where there was not much earth. The plants grew quickly, because the soil was shallow; but when the sun came up the plants were scorched because they lacked both root and moisture. Therefore they withered away and died. And some of the seeds fell among thorns. They grew, but the thorns grew more quickly and choked the tiny seedlings.

"But other seeds fell on good ground. These seeds took root and sprouted, growing into tall healthy plants that yielded up to a hundred times more seed than the sower had scattered in the first place. And I say to you, he that has ears to hear, let him hear."

Neither his disciples nor the rest of the listeners could understand what Jesus meant, although they knew that seeds would only grow in healthy soil. He explained his meaning to them. "Hear, then," he said. "The seed is the word of God, the sower is he who sows the message, and the soil is the people to whom the message is given. The wayside represents those who hear the message but do not want to act upon it. Then, as the birds fly down to eat up seeds that are scattered by the wayside, so does the evil one come to carry off the message that has been sown in their hearts.

"The stony places upon which the seeds fall and take root quickly, and then die, are like the people who receive the word with joy and gladness as soon as they hear it, but because they are shallow the word can take no root. For a while they believe, but in time of temptation or doubt they are quick to fall away.

"The thorny places refer to those people who hear the word of God and believe in their hearts, but allow the cares and riches and pleasures of this world to choke the word and crowd it out, so that their faith never ripens sufficiently to bear fruit.

"And the good ground that receives the seed represents the people who hear God's word, understand it, and obey it. When the words of God fall into willing hearts, they ripen into fruits of faith that increase like the grain that fell upon good soil."

He told them, next, a parable about good seeds and bad weeds.

"The kingdom of heaven," he said, "may be likened to a man who sowed good seeds in his field. But while he slept his enemy came and sowed weeds among the wheat, and went his way. When the blades of wheat sprang up and bore good grain, the weeds sprouted with them and quickly grew.

"The servants of the householder went to him and said: 'Sir, did you not sow good seeds in your field? Where did all the weeds come from?'

" 'An enemy has done this,' answered the man.

" 'Then,' said the servants, 'would you have us go out and gather them up?'

" 'No,' the householder replied. 'Let both wheat and weeds grow together until the time of harvest. If you pull the weeds out now you may root up the good wheat with them. At harvest time I will tell the reapers to gather the weeds first and tie them up in bundles for burning; and then to gather the wheat into the barn.' "

When Jesus had finished telling this parable his disciples were just as puzzled as before. Although they had more understanding than the other listeners, they could not be sure what Jesus meant.

"Explain to us the meaning of the parable of the weeds," they begged.

"The sower of the good seeds is the Son of man," said Jesus. "The field is the world; and the good seeds are the people of God, the children of the kingdom. But the weeds are the children of the wicked one; the enemy that sowed them is the devil. The reapers are the angels, and the time of harvest is the day that God shall separate the good from the evil, even as the farmer burns the weeds and saves the good wheat in his barn. And the barn is the kingdom of heaven."

And then Jesus said: "You might also say that the kingdom of heaven is like a grain of mustard seed which, when it is sown in the field, is the smallest of all the seeds in the earth. But when this tiny seed is planted, it grows up and becomes greater than all the herbs. It shoots out great branches and becomes a tree so large that the birds of the air may nest in its boughs and rest under their shadow. So it is with the seed of the kingdom: it is small to begin with, but the tiny seed grows into the greatest of all things.

"Again, the kingdom of heaven is like a pearl, and the man who seeks it before all other things is like a merchant who, seeking perfect pearls and finding one of great price, sells all he has to buy the perfect pearl. Thus both the pearl merchant and the seeker of heaven give up all things for the one that is most important."

Thus did Jesus talk in parables that day by the sea of Galilee.

When evening came he said to his disciples: "Come, let us cross over to the other side."

The disciples sent away the multitude and took Jesus into a boat. As they cast off they saw that, even then, the crowds were trying to follow, for many of the people got into their own boats and rowed along behind them.

Jesus was weary after his long day of teaching and he fell asleep in the gently tossing boat. When they were far out from the shore a great wind arose and churned the waters, so that the boat rocked and plunged with the buffeting of the gusts and the boiling waves. Towers of water dashed against it and over the sides to drench the disciples and their Master, and the little ship began to fill. The storm raged on, and Jesus slept. His disciples pulled at the oars with all their strength, but they made no headway against the howling wind and lashing waves. The gusts slapped at them unmercifully; the boat was becoming dangerously full of water.

But Jesus slept on. His followers did not want to waken him, yet their plight was getting desperate. At last they came to him and woke him from his sleep. "Master!" they cried. "Do you not care that we are dying?"

Jesus rose up calmly and rebuked the winds, and to the sea he said: "Peace, be still." The wind ceased, and over the sea there was a great calm.

"Why are you so full of fear?" Jesus asked his disciples. "Have you still no faith?"

But now they were fearful for another reason. They had seen their Master heal, and they had seen him cast out devils, but the miraculous calming of a storm was something they had never seen before. They were filled with awe. "What manner of man is this?" they asked each other, marveling. "Even the winds and the sea obey him!"

Afterwards, the journey safely ended, Jesus and his disciples spent some time in Gadara on the far side of the sea, healing and teaching; and then they returned by boat to Capernaum. Crowds of people were waiting for Jesus on the shore and received him gladly, for they were eager to hear his words and ask his healing help. One of the people who most urgently wanted to see him was a man named Jairus, a leader in the synagogue at Capernaum. He threw himself down at the healer's feet and begged Jesus to come to his house, for his only daughter, who was about twelve years of age, lay dying on her sickbed.

"I pray you, come with me!" Jairus begged of Jesus. "My little daughter is lying at the point of death. Come with me, I beseech you, and lay your hands upon her so that she may be healed, and live."

Jesus turned at once and went with him. The crowd followed and thronged around him, pressing close upon him so that he could scarcely move. People jostled and clutched at him from every side. Jairus watched anxiously while Jesus made slow progress to his house, hampered in his every move. "Hurry, hurry!" thought Jairus to himself, although he did not speak the words aloud. "My daughter may be dead before we get there."

But it was impossible for anyone to hurry through the narrow, crowded streets. And even while Jairus waited, fighting back his anxiety, there was an unusual delay.

In the crowd there was a woman who had been

trying desperately to reach Jesus and beg him for his help. For twelve years she had suffered many things from her illness and from all the doctors she had gone to, but she had grown worse instead of better. By this time she had spent all she had on physicians and medicines. When she heard the things concerning Jesus she followed after him, pressing her way though the crowd to get closer to the healer. "If I may but touch his clothes," she was saying to herself, "I will be healed." And she had no doubt at all that this was so.

At last she came close enough so that she could reach out and touch the border of his robe. Immediately she felt her illness leave her, and she let others in the crowd push past her to throng around the Master.

Jesus looked around. "Who was that who touched my robe?" he asked.

"It is not possible to say who touched you," his disciples answered. "You see the multitude pressing all around you. How can you say, 'Who touched me?'"

"I know someone with faith has touched me," Jesus answered, "for I felt the healing spirit flow from my body to another's." And he looked about to see the person who had touched him and been cured.

When the woman saw that she could not escape his notice, she came forward and threw herself down at Jesus' feet. Trembling with awe and wonder, knowing what had happened within her, she told him before all the people why she had touched his robe and how she had been healed immediately.

"Daughter, your faith has made you whole," Jesus said gently. "Go in peace."

Before he had finished talking to her a messenger came from the house of Jairus and pushed his way through the crowd toward the leader of the synagogue. "Your daughter is dead," the messenger said. "Trouble the Master no more, for she is gone."

Jairus cried out in his grief. But Jesus had heard what the messenger had said and he turned to the sorrowing Jairus. "Do not be afraid," he said. "Only believe, and she will be made well."

When at last he arrived at the house of Jairus he motioned the crowd to stay outside, for they were still following him and would have pushed in after him if he had permitted it, and he went inside with Peter, James, and John. Mourners had already gathered to bewail the little girl's death. The house was a tumult of weeping and wailing. Jesus looked around at all the moaning people and said: "Why do you weep and make this noise? Do not weep; the little girl is not dead, she only sleeps."

With that the mourners ceased their lamentations long enough to laugh scornfully at Jesus, for they knew the girl was dead. They had seen her lifeless body. But Jesus firmly sent them out of the house and went into the little girl's room with her father and mother and his three disciples.

He looked down at her where she lay and took her by the hand. And then he spoke. "Little maid, I say to you—arise!"

She opened her eyes and looked up into the smiling face of Jesus. And she got up at once and walked about the room.

"Now give her something to eat," said Jesus. Her parents nodded dumbly, for they were grateful and astonished beyond words.

Jesus left the house of Jairus and went back to the waiting crowd.

There were many more crowds awaiting him as he traveled through the cities and the villages, so many that he said to his disciples one day: "They are distressed and scattered, as sheep that do not have a shepherd. See, the harvest indeed is plenteous, but the laborers are few." And he called to him his chosen twelve apostles and began to send them forth two by two that they might do his work abroad. He gave them healing power, and authority over the unclean spirits that they might cast them out, and then he said to them:

"Go now, and preach that the kingdom of heaven is at hand. Heal the sick, raise the dead, cleanse the lepers, cast out demons; receive with thanks, and freely give. Take nothing for your journey save a staff, and the robe and sandals that you wear. Take neither wallet, silver, gold, nor extra coat. Stay wherever you are made welcome, and bless the house that receives you and is worthy. Wherever you are not made welcome and your words are not received, leave that house or town and shake off the dust of it from beneath your feet. Have faith, and fear not—but beware of men. For they will deliver you up to their councils, and in their synagogues they will scourge you."

When he had finished commanding his disciples he went his way to teach alone, and they went forth by twos to preach and heal in the countryside and villages.

Now at that time Herod the tetrarch heard of all these things that were being done by Jesus and his twelve disciples, and he was very much perplexed. He had heard of the so-called "King of the Jews" and wondered if this Jesus might not be the man. On the other hand, it was said by some that it was John the Baptist risen from the dead. Others said that Elijah had reappeared on earth, and yet others suggested the names of other old prophets who might have risen again.

Herod thought about it long and hard. At last he said: "It is John, whom I beheaded; he is risen again!" Yet he was not quite sure, and went on asking: "Who is this, about whom I hear such things?"

And he became increasingly anxious to see this man about whom he kept hearing such strange and wonderful things.

# The Feeding
## of the Multitude

✴✴✴✴✴✴✴✴✴✴✴✴✴✴✴✴✴✴✴✴✴✴✴

After all these events and many others the disciples gathered together and returned to Jesus. They told him all that they had done, and he was pleased.

"Come, let us go into a desert place," he said, "so that we may rest a while." For there had been so much coming and going of people that neither Jesus nor his disciples had had time enough even to eat.

They took a boat across the sea of Galilee to search out a place where they might have some little time to themselves. But even in the desert place they could not rest. When people discovered where Jesus had gone they followed in their boats or hurried around by land from all the neighboring towns and villages, so that a multitude was gathered on the far shore even before Jesus arrived.

And Jesus, when he saw them there, had compassion for them. He bade them welcome and began to speak to them of the kingdom of God. As the day wore on he answered those with questions and healed all those who needed healing, and he taught them many things. The afternoon grew late, and yet the people stayed on, listening, in their hundreds and their thousands.

When it was almost evening his disciples came to him and said, "There is no food in this desert place, and it is very late. Let us send these people away so that they may go into the farms and villages round about and buy themselves something to eat."

"They have no need to go away," said Jesus. "We will give them food." Then he turned to his disciple Philip. "Where shall we buy bread, that all these people may eat?" he asked. This he said to test Philip, for he himself knew what he would do.

Philip shook his head. The disciples had very little money between them, and the crowd was immense. "Two hundred pennyworth of bread would not be enough for all these people," he said, "even if each one only took a little."

"Then go and see how many loaves you can find among the people," Jesus said.

His disciples went through the crowd inquiring of the people. Finally Andrew, Simon Peter's brother, came back and reported what he had found.

"There is a lad here who has a basket with five barley loaves and two fishes," he said. "But what is that, among so many?"

"Bring the loaves and fishes here," said Jesus, "and have the people sit down on the grass in groups of fifty and a hundred."

Andrew brought the basket to him. And all the people, about five thousand of them, sat down upon the grass in groups. Jesus took the five loaves and two fishes and, looking up to heaven, gave a blessing. He broke first the loaves and then the fishes into small pieces and gave them to his disciples to distribute to the people. All the people ate, and all were filled. There seemed to be no end to the fragments of food.

When everyone had had enough to eat, Jesus said to his disciples: "Now gather up the fragments that remain, so that nothing shall be wasted." So the disciples gathered up the food that was left, filling twelve baskets with what remained after all the five thousand men, women, and children had eaten their fill.

Excitement ran through the crowd as they realized what had happened. Many of them said, "This is indeed the prophet who was to come into the world! It is he who is meant to be our king!" As Jesus looked at them he saw what they were thinking, and he knew that they wanted to carry him off and make him their earthly king. But the kingdom of Jesus was not of this world and he could not allow them to do what they were thinking, so he told his disciples to get into the boat and cross before him toward Capernaum on the other side of the sea while he himself sent all the people away.

When all the others had gone, the multitude as well as his disciples, Jesus went up the mountain alone to pray.

When night came he was still praying alone, high on the mountainside. His disciples were well on their way across the inland sea to Capernaum. But high, gusty winds had come with the darkness, and the little ship was tossing about in the midst of a growing storm. Jesus came down from the mountain and stood alone on the shore, watching his disciples in their distant battle with the waves. After a while he went toward them on the sea, walking across the water as if it had been solid land beneath his feet.

The disciples looked up from their rowing when they saw the shadowy figure coming toward them through the night. And at the sight of someone walking on the water they nearly dropped their oars with fear. They had seen strange things, but none so strange as this, and at first they did not even think that the figure might be their leader Jesus.

"It is a spirit!" they cried out in their terror.

"Be of good cheer!" Jesus said at once. "It is I. Do not be afraid."

"If it is indeed you, Lord," said Peter, "Then let me come toward you on the water."

"Come!" said Jesus.

Peter stepped bravely from the tossing boat onto the surface of the water and began to walk. But when the strong wind blew against him, and churned the seas beneath his feet, he suddenly became afraid. He felt his feet go under; he felt his big, strong body beginning to sink. "Lord, save me!" he cried out.

Jesus stretched out his hand and caught him.

"O ye of little faith!" he said. "Why did you doubt?"

And Jesus guided Peter to the boat across the foaming sea and helped him climb aboard.

The wind ceased at once, and they went along their way. Again his disciples were amazed by his extraordinary powers, for even the miracle of the loaves and fishes had not taught them what manner of being they had in their midst. Now they worshiped him, and said: "You are in truth the Son of God!" Yet they still said it more in awe than in true belief.

Nevertheless, they thought these things as they crossed the sea on calm waters and continued with their mission on the other side; and they thought about them as they traveled with Jesus from Galilee to Phoenicia and back again to Palestine. Simon Peter, in particular, was very thoughtful while they journeyed. Finally, Jesus and the twelve made their way to Caesarea Philippi at the foot of great Mount Hermon.

On the way he questioned his disciples.

"Who do people say I am?" he asked.

"Some say you are John the Baptist," they answered, "and some say you are Elijah. Yet others say that you are Jeremiah, or another of the old prophets that has risen again."

"But who do you say that I am?" asked Jesus.

And Simon Peter answered, saying: "You are the Christ, the Son of the living God!"

Jesus rejoiced when he heard Peter's words. "Blessed are you, Simon, son of Jona!" he said. "For flesh and blood has not told you this, but my Father who is in heaven. And I say to you that you are Peter, the rock,

and upon this rock I will build my church." Now he
knew that his disciples, or at least one of them, believed
him to be the promised Christ. But he also knew that
other people did not yet believe it, and he wanted them
to find out for themselves. So he commanded his disciples to tell no one that he was the Christ.

He began to teach them, then, about what the future
held in store.

"I will go to Jerusalem," he said, "and suffer many
things at the hands of the elders and chief priests and
scribes. All of them will reject me and abuse me. I shall
be killed, but after three days I will rise again."

They were shocked at what they heard. Peter took
his Master aside and reproved him for saying such
things, for he was convinced that Jesus could prevent
the fate he was foretelling. It was true; Jesus had the
power to prevent what lay ahead. But it was God's plan
that his Son should bear the burden of man's sins.

"It can not be, Lord!" Peter said. "Such things must
never happen to you!"

"You are talking like Satan the tempter," Jesus said
to him. "It will be as I say. You shall not be a stum-
bling block to me in the things I have to do. Still you
do not understand, for you are thinking man's
thoughts, not the thoughts of God."

They traveled on in silence for some time. Then
Jesus said to his disciples: "If any man wishes to come
after me, let him deny all worldly desires, and take up
his cross, and follow me. He is not to live selfishly, but
for the Lord his God. For whoever wishes to save his
life shall lose it, but whoever gives up his life for my
sake, and for the sake of the gospel, will be saved. For
what shall it profit a man to gain the whole world
and lose his own soul? Or what shall a man give in
exchange for his soul? Is there anything of equal value?
I say to you, there is not! But God will reward each
man according to what he does."

Six days later, Jesus took Peter, James, and John up
Mount Hermon with him to pray. And as he prayed

the expression of his face was changed and his whole appearance glowed. His face shone like the sun; his garments became as bright as white and glittering snow.

Two men appeared to talk to him: not his disciples, and not men of the earth, but Moses and Elijah in all their heavenly glory. And they spoke to him about the death awaiting him in Jerusalem.

Peter and those who were with him were heavy with sleep and did not hear the talk. But when they awoke they saw the glory of Jesus and the two figures with him, and Peter knew who they were. He cried out: "Master, it is good that we are here! If you will, let us make three tabernacles; one for you, and one for Moses, and one for Elijah!" But he scarcely knew what he was saying, so dumbfounded was he by the amazing sight.

As he spoke a bright cloud came and overshadowed them, drawing them into its midst. Out of it there came a voice that said: "This is my beloved Son, in whom I am well pleased. Hear him!"

The disciples fell on their faces in fear. Jesus came to them through the brightness of the cloud and touched them. "Rise up," he said. "Do not be afraid."

When they looked up the cloud was gone, and they were alone on the mountain with Jesus. Of the two heavenly visitors there was no sign.

As they came down from the mountain Jesus told them to tell no one about the vision they had seen, not until after he had risen from the dead.

They kept it a secret to themselves, but they questioned among themselves what Jesus had meant by "rising from the dead."

He had said it before, and he would say it again. And in time to come they would find out what he meant.

# Disputes
# in the Temple

❦❦❦❦❦❦❦❦❦❦❦❦❦❦❦❦❦❦❦❦❦❦❦

Jesus and his disciples left Caesarea Philippi and made their way back to Capernaum in Galilee. As they traveled he tried again to teach them about the future and explain what had been talked about upon the mountainside while Peter, James, and John lay heavy with sleep.

"Let these words sink into your ears," Jesus said, "for the Son of man shall be betrayed into the hands of men, and they will kill him. But on the third day after his death he will rise again."

Yet the words did not sink in. The twelve could not bring themselves to believe that Jesus would allow himself to die; not with his great power to save and heal. They thought, therefore, that he was speaking in a parable, and they were afraid to ask him what he meant.

Jesus walked on, alone with his thoughts. His disciples drew apart from him and began an earnest discussion with one another, glancing now and then at Jesus as they spoke. He was not listening to them.

All this while they could have talked about the meaning of his saying, or what had happened on the mountain, or how it was possible for a man to rise after being three days dead; but they talked of nothing of the sort. They talked about themselves.

When they arrived at Capernaum they went at once to Simon Peter's house, which Jesus had called home ever since his own town of Nazareth had rejected him. After they had all refreshed themselves, Jesus sat down and called his disciples to him, for he knew what had been in their hearts while they were talking on the road to Capernaum. The twelve joined him where he sat.

"What was it that you disputed among yourselves along the way?" he asked. They were ashamed to answer, for they had been arguing about which one of them would be the greatest in the kingdom of heaven. They were still under the impression that it would be a kingdom similar to those on earth, and that Jesus would be appointing them to various high positions. And they were silent, for whatever else they failed to understand they did know that Jesus had no sympathy for worldly ambitions.

Jesus waited. Then he said: "If any man desires to be first in the kingdom, he must make himself the least of all and the servant of all. For if anyone is to be great, he must serve not himself, but others."

Now there were children in the household, and Jesus called a little child to come to him. The little one came gladly and Jesus put his arms about him. "Unless you change and become again like little children," he said to his disciples, "you will never enter the kingdom of heaven. Whoever, therefore, shall humble himself as this little child, shall be the greatest in the kingdom of heaven. And I say to you also, that whoever shall welcome one such child in my name, receives me also and makes me welcome. And whoever welcomes me receives not only me but also the Father who sent me. But whoever causes any one of the little ones who believe in me to waver in his faith, to turn aside and stumble, let that man beware: it would be better for him to have a millstone hung around his neck and to be

sunk in the depth of the sea than to face the wrath of
our Father in heaven. Do not despise one single little
child! For it is not the will of my Father in heaven
that any of these little ones should perish by going astray."

Jesus loved little children and their purity of heart.
He sought them out to talk to them; and he welcomed
them whenever they came to him. There was to come a
time in Jerusalem when he would be so surrounded by
children that he could scarcely teach their elders. On
that day, it seemed that all the mothers in the city had
brought their youngsters and their babies so that Jesus
might put his hands on them and bless them. Then his
disciples, exasperated by the endless procession of eager
little ones, rebuked those who brought their children to
see Jesus. Somehow they had decided for themselves
that Jesus was much too busy to give his time to them.
Yet they were wrong, for Jesus was never too busy to
welcome children. He wanted them to come to him,
and they themselves loved to gather around to touch his
robe and listen to his stories. But the disciples reproved
the mothers who had brought them. Jesus was much
displeased when he saw them trying to keep the little
ones away.

"Let the children come to me!" he said. "Forbid
them not, for the kingdom of heaven belongs to such as
they. I tell you again, whoever shall not accept the
kingdom of God just like a little child, shall not enter
into it at all. Now bring them here." And he took the
little ones into his arms to bless them.

That, however, was later. At the moment, Jerusalem
still lay ahead, for the feast of the tabernacles was at
hand, and Jesus had decided to go to the temple to
worship and teach. He did not want to call attention to
his arrival, and he sent his disciples ahead while he
himself visited his friends, Mary, Martha, and Lazarus
in the little town of Bethany on the outskirts of
Jerusalem. When he did go into the city he went late
and secretly.

The Jews therefore sought him at the feast. "Where is he?" they asked each other. No one knew but there was much murmuring among the multitudes concerning him. Some said, "He is a good man." Others said, "No, not so! He leads the multitude astray." No one of the masses spoke openly about him for fear of the leaders among the Jews.

In the midst of the festival Jesus went up into the temple and taught with the authority that made him so different from all other teachers. The Jews marveled at his sayings. "How is it that this man is so learned, never having been taught?" they asked each other. Jesus heard, and answered.

"The teaching is not mine," he said, "but his that sent me. Anyone who truly desires to do God's will shall know whether my teaching comes from God, or only from myself." And he went on teaching them.

His listeners were amazed at his logic and at the truths he spoke.

"Is not this he whom the leaders seek to kill?" one man asked another. "He speaks so openly, and they say nothing to him! Can it be that the rulers indeed *know* that this is the Christ? But no, he cannot be! We know this man, this Nazarene; when the Christ comes, no one will know where he is from."

Many of the multitude believed in him, nevertheless, and they murmured much among themselves. "When Christ does come," they said to one another, "can he possibly show more signs than this man has done?" The Pharisees heard what the masses were saying. Now, they thought, they would have their opportunity to arrest the man who spoke so unflatteringly of them and their strict adherence to the Law. They were still smarting over his comments on their public humility and private sin, and they had had enough. So, together with the chief priests, they decided to have him arrested immediately.

A band of officers therefore trooped into the temple to seize Jesus and take him to their masters. Instead of

the fiery radical they expected, they found a
calm-faced man speaking in a quiet but compelling
voice to a crowd of fascinated listeners. "I will be with
you for yet a little while," the man was saying. "And
when I go, I go to him that sent me. You shall look for
me, but will not find me. Where I am, you cannot
come."

At this there was a discussion within the crowd.
Where could he possibly go, that they would be unable
to follow? Abroad, perhaps?

The officers who had come to take him hung back
and listened, both to the crowd and to the words of this
extraordinary man. They heard him say such things as:
'If any man thirst, let him come to me and drink!"
and, "I am the light of the world! Whoever follows me
will not have to walk in darkness, but will live his life
in the light."

They saw how eagerly the people listened, and they
took note of the response of the multitude. Some said,
"Of a truth, this is the prophet!" Others said, "This is
the Christ." And others yet: "This is *not* the Christ, for
this man comes from Galilee. Was not the Christ to
have been born in Bethlehem?" So the people were
divided in their opinions about Jesus, and the officers
themselves did not know what to think. They tried to
do their duty, but for some reason they were unable to
lay their hands upon Jesus. Indeed, they found themselves not only interested but moved by his words.
They went back to the chief priests and Pharisees without the captive they had been sent to get. Their masters
were very much annoyed.

"Why have you not brought him?" they demanded.

"No man ever talked as he does!" the officers replied.

"Are you also led astray?" the Pharisees said angrily.
"Do you now believe in him? Tell us: have any of the
authorities believed in him, or any of the Pharisees?
No! Only the common people, the multitude that does
not know the Law, believe in him—and for that they

are accursed! And this man, you can be sure, will be punished yet for his heretical teachings."

Now Nicodemus, the man who had gone secretly to see Jesus many months before and had been deeply impressed by what he heard, was sitting among his fellow Pharisees while they spoke thus about Jesus. And he did not like the things that they were saying.

"Does our Law condemn a man before he is given a hearing?" he asked.

"A hearing!" they said scornfully. "We know what he has done. What is the matter with you? Are you from Galilee, too? Search through the writings, and you will see that no prophet is to come from Galilee!"

After this they were even more determined to find some way of trapping Jesus into admitting that he was guilty of breaking their Law.

Jesus knew that his days were numbered. Yet he still came and went as he pleased, preaching as he knew he must preach and doing those things that he knew he must do.

One sabbath day, as Jesus and his disciples were walking in Jerusalem, they saw a beggar who had been blind from birth.

As they drew near the disciples said to Jesus, "Master, who sinned, that this man should have been born blind? Was it he who sinned, or was it his parents?" For the Jews thought that all misfortune was caused by someone's sin.

They stopped in front of the blind man.

"He did not sin, nor did his parents," Jesus answered; and the blind man raised his sightless eyes as if the better to hear the gentle voice. "He was born blind so that the power of God might be shown through him. And we must use this power, do God's work, while it is still day; for the night is coming when no man can work. As long as I am in this world, I am the light of the world."

When Jesus had said this he spat on the ground, and made clay from the earth and the spittle. Then he anointed the man's eyes with clay and said to him, "Go, wash your eyes in the Pool of Siloam."

The blind man arose and made his way through the city streets and out through the gate of Jerusalem to the Pool of Siloam, knowing his way though he had never seen the road. He felt his way down to the water and washed as Jesus had bidden him. The clay came away from his eyes; he opened them; and for the first time in his life he was able to see. Incredulously, only half believing even yet, he ran up the hill from the pool and hurried home to tell his parents the wonderful news. His heart sang as he ran, and his newly opened eyes looked with delight upon everything they saw.

He was well known in Jerusalem, this blind man, for he was to be seen every day begging in the street. And when his neighbors, and other people who had seen him sitting by the roadside with his hands outstretched, saw him running to his house with eyes wide open and a joyous smile upon his face, they were astonished.

"Is not this the man who used to sit and beg?" they asked each other.

Some said, "Yes, it is he!"

But others said, "No, it cannot be. It is someone like him."

The blind man spoke for himself. "I *am* he!" he said.

"How, then, were your eyes opened?" they asked, in their astonishment.

"The man who is named Jesus made clay," he answered them, "and put it on my eyes. Then I went to wash them in the Pool of Siloam, as he said I must, and I received my sight!"

His astounded neighbors brought him before the Pharisees, who questioned him. He repeated his story to them. And they muttered angrily because again the cure had taken place on a sabbath day.

Some of them said: "The man who did this is not a man of God, because he does not keep the sabbath."

But others said: "How could a sinner do such a miracle as this?"

And there was a division of opinion among the people who heard and talked about all this. Therefore they asked the once-blind man what he himself thought about the one who had opened his eyes.

"He is a prophet!" he answered.

Then the questioning Jews would not believe that the man had actually been blind and had been given his sight. They therefore sent him out of hearing and summoned his parents to question them as well.

"Is this your son, and was he indeed born blind?" they asked. "If so, how is it that he now can see?"

"Yes, this is our son, and we know he was born blind," his parents answered. "But how it is that he now can see, we do not know." They did know, for he had told them and they believed his words. But they denied knowledge because they feared the Jewish authorities, for the Jews had already announced that anyone who acknowledged Jesus as the Christ would be turned out of the synagogue. Therefore they said, "Ask our son. He is of age. Let him speak for himself."

Then the Pharisees again summoned the man who had been blind.

"Give the glory to God for what has happened to you," they told him, "for we know that the man you say has done this thing is a sinner."

"Whether he is a sinner or not I do not know," the man replied. "But one thing I do know: I was blind, and now I can see."

His answer displeased them mightily.

"What did he do to you?" they persisted. "How did he open your eyes?"

"I have already told you, and you would not listen," he said. "Why do you want to hear it again? Do you wish to become his disciples?"

"Pah! *You* are his disciple," they said angrily, "but we are disciples of Moses. We know that God spoke to Moses. But as for this man, we do not know that God has spoken to him; we do not know where he is from."

"Why, that is very strange," the man said. "You know nothing of him, you who claim to know so much, and yet he made me see! Now we know that God does not listen to sinners, but if a man worships God and obeys him, God does listen to him. It has never been heard, since the world began, that anyone has opened the eyes of a man born blind. If this man were not from God, he could do no such thing."

The Pharisees turned on him in anger. "You were born in sin and you are altogether sinful! And do you now try to teach us, you sinner?" And they cast him out of the synagogue so that he would never again be allowed to worship there and be accepted as a true believer in their God.

But the man born blind did not need to worship there. When Jesus heard how the Pharisees had treated him he sought him out and spoke to him.

"Do you believe in the Son of God?" he asked.

"Who is he, that I may believe in him?" the man asked in return.

"You have seen him," Jesus answered. "It is he who speaks with you."

"Lord, I believe!" the man said joyfully. He fell to his knees and worshiped Jesus. And although from that time forth he was no longer welcome in the synagogue, he prayed within his heart and knew that his prayers were being heard.

# The Gathering Storm

✦✦✦✦✦✦✦✦✦✦✦✦✦✦✦✦✦✦✦✦✦✦✦✦

In spite of the growing hatred and plotting of the Pharisees, Jesus went quietly on with his work. Soon after healing the blind man, Jesus spoke again in parables to the people of Jerusalem and the places round about.

He began with the story of the good shepherd.

"In truth, I say to you," he told his listeners, "that if anyone does not enter the sheepfold by way of the door, but tries to climb in some other way, he is a thief and a robber. The one who enters by the door is the true shepherd of the sheep. The watchman opens the door to him, and the sheep listen to his voice. The shepherd calls to his own sheep by name, for he knows them well, and leads them out to pasture. And when he has led out his sheep he goes in front of them to lead the way. They obey him and they follow him because they know his voice. But they will not follow a stranger. No, they will flee from him, because they do not know the voice of strangers."

His listeners did not understand this parable, so Jesus said: "I am the door of the sheepfold, and you, the people, are the sheep. All those who try to enter the sheepfold without waiting for the doorkeeper to open the gate are thieves and robbers; they are the false teachers who try to call my sheep. But the sheep, not knowing their voices, will not listen to them. Yes, I am the door, and the only door. Whoever enters through me shall be saved. He shall go in and go out, and he will find rich pastures. The thief comes to steal, and kill, and destroy; but I have come so that my sheep may have life, and have it in abundance.

"Or let us say, instead, that I am the good shepherd: the good shepherd lays down his life for his sheep. He that is hired, whose sheep are not his own, will not lay down his life for any of the flock. No, when the wolf comes, the hired shepherd leaves the sheep and flees; and the wolf snatches them and scatters them about.

"The false teacher is the hireling who cares not for the sheep. But I am the good shepherd: I know my sheep, and my sheep know me, even as the Father knows me and I know the Father. I will gather my sheep to me and guard every one of them. And other sheep I have, which are not of this fold. These are the Gentiles, and these, also, must I lead. They will hear my voice, and they will join the fold. Then shall there be one flock and one shepherd. And for my flock I will lay down my life.

"Therefore does the Father love me, because I am laying down my life so that I may take it back again. No one is taking it from me; I am giving it of myself. I have power to give it, and I have power to take it back. This is the authority I have received from my Father."

Again there arose a division of opinion among the Jews because of these words. They could not understand everything he said, but they did understand that he had spoken of God as his Father.

Many of them said, "He is possessed by a demon! He is mad! Why do you listen to him?"

But others said, "These are not the words of a man who is possessed. And can a madman open the eyes of the blind?"

Jesus went his way, leaving them to their argument.

One day, while he was teaching, a certain expert in the Law got up to test him with hard questions, hoping to be able to trick Jesus into saying something that the Pharisees might use against him.

"Master," he said, "what shall I do to inherit eternal life?"

"Can you not answer that yourself?" said Jesus. "You know the Law. What is written in it? How do you read it?"

The lawyer answered, "In the Law of Moses it is written: 'You shall love the Lord your God with all your heart, and with all your soul, and with all your strength, and with all your mind; and you shall love your neighbor as yourself.' "

"You have answered rightly," Jesus said. "Do this, and you shall have eternal life. For these are the greatest of the commandments."

His answer showed that he had come to uphold the Law rather than destroy it, but the lawyer was not satisfied.

"But who is my neighbor?" the man persisted.

Jesus answered with a parable.

"One day," he said, "a certain man was traveling the road from Jerusalem to Jericho. On the way he fell among thieves, who attacked him brutally and robbed him of everything he had. They stripped him, beat him, and departed, leaving him half dead.

"He lay there on the side of the road, bruised, bleeding, unable to move, and praying that help would come before he died.

"Now a priest chanced to be going that way, and he saw the wounded man lying by the side of the road. The man glimpsed the priest through his half-closed eyes, and he thought, 'Surely he will help me!' But the priest crossed the road and went past on the other side, making no move to help or even stop.

"And then a Levite came traveling down the road. He, too, saw the beaten man and heard his moans; and he, too, crossed over and passed by on the other side.

"At last there came a Samaritan." His audience stirred and made disdainful faces, for they despised Samaritans. "He rode up to the man," Jesus continued, "and saw his pitiful plight. And his heart was moved with deep compassion. He dismounted at once and bent over the wounded traveler. What the man was or where he came from made no difference to this Samaritan: all he thought of was that the man was suffering and desperately in need of help. He could see that, unless he were attended to at once, the man would surely die.

"Therefore the Samaritan dressed the wounds with wine and oil, and bound them up as best he could. Then he raised the man up with gentle, kindly hands and lifted him onto his own mule, for the man's mount had been stolen with all the rest of his possessions.

"The Samaritan led his mule and its burden along the road to Jericho until he reached the safety of an inn. There he lifted off the wounded man and gave him shelter; and he cared for him in the inn throughout the night. And in the morning, when he was ready to depart and attend to his own delayed affairs, he took money from his own wallet and gave it to the innkeeper. 'Take care of this man,' he said, 'and if you spend more on him than this, 'I will repay you when I come back.' And then he left.

"Now," said Jesus, "which of the three, do you think, proved himself a neighbor to that man who fell into the hands of thieves: the priest, the Levite, or the Samaritan?"

"The one who showed mercy to him," the lawyer said reluctantly.

"Yes," said Jesus. "Go, and do the same yourself."

And the lawyer departed from his presence, a little humbler and a little wiser.

It was some time later in the winter, that Jesus again attended a festival in Jerusalem. He was walking in the temple during the feast of dedication when the people saw him and surrounded him on Solomon's Porch.

"How much longer are you going to keep us in suspense?" they demanded. "If you really are the Christ, then tell us plainly!"

"I told you," Jesus answered them, "and you would not believe me. The deeds that I do in my Father's name are proof of my words. But you do not hear me and believe, because you are not of my sheep, as I said to you. My sheep listen to my voice: I know them, and they follow me. I give them eternal life; they shall never die, or be plucked out of my hands. My Father who gave them to me is greater than all, and no one is able to snatch them out of my Father's hands. And my Father and I are one."

Now he had said it! He had as much as said he was the Father himself! The Jews in the temple were outraged. They shouted angrily and picked up stones with the intention of stoning him to death in the heat of their rage, but he stood calmly before them without a trace of fear.

"Why do you do this?" Jesus asked them. "I have shown you many good works from the Father. For which of those works are you stoning me?"

"We are not stoning you for any good work," they answered roughly, "but for your impious talk; and because you, a man, are making yourself out to be God. This is blasphemy!"

"How can you say I am blasphemous," said Jesus, "when my Father has sanctified me and sent me as his messenger to the world? If I am not doing my Father's work, do not believe in me. But if I am doing his work, even though you may not believe in me, then at least believe in the deeds. By these deeds you may come to know and understand that the Father is in me and I am in the Father."

They were not calmed by his words. They tried again to hurt and seize him, but he escaped from their hands and went away.

Again, he went across the Jordan to the place where John had first baptized, and there he stayed for a time.

Many people came to see him and his miraculous signs; and many people grew to believe in him.

Now the Pharisees were still on the lookout for him, listening to his words and complaining about him to each other, but they did not dare to harm him as long as he was across the Jordan from Judea. Many publicans and sinners were drawing near to Jesus to listen to his words, so both the Pharisees and the accompanying scribes murmured angrily among themselves and said: "This man welcomes sinners. He even eats with them!"

"Yes, I welcome sinners," Jesus said. "It is the sinners who need me, every single one of them. And it is the sinners who shall be received when they seek me." Again, he began to speak in parables.

"What man among you," he began, "if he has a hundred sheep, would be satisfied if one should stray and leave him with only ninety-nine? If one is lost, would you leave that one in the wilderness, or would you go out after it and search until you had found it? You search for it, I say; you do not leave it in the wilderness. And when you find it, you lay it across your shoulders and carry it to the fold, rejoicing. When you reach home you call together your friends and neighbors and you say to them: 'Rejoice with me! For I have found my lost sheep.' And I say to you, there will be more joy in heaven over one sinner who repents than over ninety-nine righteous people who do not need to repent."

He spoke another parable. "What woman who has ten pieces of silver, and loses one, will not light a lamp and sweep the house and look diligently until she finds it? And when she finds it, does she not call in her friends and neighbors, saying, 'Rejoice with me, for I have found the coin I lost!' In just that way, I say to you, there is joy among the angels of God over one single sinner who repents."

And then again he said: "There was a certain man who had two sons. The elder was righteous, and occupied with serious thoughts. The younger was carefree and reckless, eager to enjoy the pleasures that his inheritance would bring him. 'Father,' he said one day, when he could wait no longer, 'let me have my share of the property that is coming to me. Let me enjoy it now.' His father was not pleased, but he divided his property into two portions and gave his younger son the share that would have come to him in later years.

"Not many days afterward, the younger son gathered together all his possessions and new wealth and journeyed into a far country. There he spent gloriously and lived a riotous life with greedy new friends and women companions. It was not long before he had squandered away all his inheritance. When all his money was gone his new friends left him too, so that there was no one to help him in his time of need.

"Then a mighty famine came upon the land, and he began to be in desperate want. He who had once lived in luxury and spent foolishly was now forced to accept the only work he could find, that of laborer to one of the citizens of that country. The man was a farmer, and he sent the youth into his fields to feed the swine.

"The new swineherd did his work, but though he worked he was given nothing in return. His hunger grew unbearable. After a while he would gladly have filled his belly with the husks that were given to the swine.

"Then he came to his senses and began to think. 'How many hired men my father has,' he thought, 'who have food enough and to spare, and I am dying here of hunger!' He thought about his home, and it became more and more attractive as he thought. Yet could he admit that he had been wrong and go back to his father? He decided that he could, for self-pride was not important to a man in his condition. And he truly repented of the foolish things that he had done. 'I will arise, I will leave here,' he told himself, 'and go back to my father. I will say to him, Father, I have sinned against heaven and against you. I am no more worthy to be called your son. Treat me, if you will, as one of your hired servants; only let me come home again.'

"He started on his journey home and eventually approached his father's house, worrying all the while about how he would be received and grieving for his foolishness. And his father, who had missed him and was concerned for him, saw him when he was still a long way off. As the youth drew closer the father saw that his son was ragged and dirty, completely without possessions and walking with his head bowed low. Love and compassion stirred within the older man. He ran from the house and threw his arms around his son, and kissed him with a joyous father's kisses.

"The youth was ashamed and drew away from him. 'Father, I have sinned against heaven, and in your sight,' he said. 'I am no longer worthy to be called your son. Let me be as one of your hired—'

"But his father would not let him finish. 'Bring forth the best robe!' he called to his servants. 'Put it on my son, and put a ring on his finger, and shoes on his feet. Bring the fatted calf; prepare a feast! Let us eat and make merry, for this my son was as if dead and is alive again; he was lost, and he is found!'

"The household began at once to make merry. The youth was brought fresh clothes, the finest in the house; the calf was prepared, and the wine jars opened. Now while all this was happening the elder son was working diligently in the fields. When he returned to the homestead after a day's work he heard the sounds of music and dancing coming from the house. He called to one of the servants and inquired into the cause of the unusual merriment.

" 'What is the meaning of all this?' he asked.

" 'Your brother has come back,' the servant answered happily, 'and your father has killed the fatted calf because the youth has come back safe and sound.'

"But the brother was angry instead of being glad, and he would not go into the house to take part in the celebration. His father therefore came out to him and urged him to come in to welcome his brother and join the feast. Still the older brother could not feel happy for his father.

" 'I have served you all these years,' he said angrily, 'and never once have I disobeyed a commandment of yours nor spent money foolishly. Yet you have never given me so much as an unfattened kid of a goat, that I might make merry with my friends. No, you do not rejoice over me! But as soon as your other son comes back, he who has wasted your money on loose women and riotous women, you kill for him the calf you have been fattening! Is this fair, is it right?'

"And the father saw that he was jealous. 'Son,' he said gently, 'you are always with me; you have not been away, you have not strayed. Everything I have is yours. But it is only right to make merry and be glad, for your brother who was dead has come back to life; he was lost, and now he is found! Come, rejoice with us.'

"And in this way," Jesus ended quietly, "does my Father welcome each sinner who repents and comes to him. And thus do I welcome all sinners who repent and come to me."

# The Raising
## of Lazarus

✦✦✦✦✦✦✦✦✦✦✦✦✦✦✦✦✦✦✦✦✦✦✦

While Jesus was still in the land beyond the Jordan
he received an urgent call for help from his friends in
Bethany. Mary, Martha, and their brother Lazarus
loved Jesus dearly, and he loved them in return. He
had made it his custom to visit them whenever he was
near Jerusalem, for with them he always found friendship, hospitality, and true belief.

And now Mary and Martha had sent a message to
him, saying, "Lord! Behold, Lazarus, whom you love,
is very ill."

Now Jesus was many miles away from Bethany and
it took time for the message to reach him. Indeed, when
the messenger at last found Jesus where he taught,
Lazarus was already on the point of death. Yet even
then the Master did not hurry off to Bethany.

"This sickness is not unto death," he said. "It is for
the glory of God, that the Son of God may be glorified
thereby."

The messenger went his way and Jesus went on with
his teaching. His disciples were glad that he was making no attempt to go to Bethany, for Judea was no
longer safe for him. Therefore they made no objection

as he continued preaching and healing among the people of the land beyond the Jordan.

Meanwhile, in Bethany, Lazarus grew sicker yet; and, while his sisters watched and wept, he died.

Two days later Jesus said to his disciples: "Let us go back to Judea."

"Master!" they protested. "The leaders of the Jews were but recently trying to stone you. And still you want to go there again?"

"Yes, I am going," he answered. "Our friend Lazarus has fallen asleep. I am going so that I might wake him from his sleep."

"Lord," the disciples said to him, "if he has fallen asleep, he surely will recover."

Now Jesus had spoken of his friend's death, but they thought he meant that Lazarus was taking rest in sleep and was therefore on the road to health.

"Lazarus is dead," Jesus told them plainly. "And I am glad for your sakes that I was not there, so that you may learn to believe in me. Come, let us go to him."

Jesus and his disciples arrived in Bethany two days later and found that Lazarus had been in the tomb for four days already. A number of Jews had come out from nearby Jerusalem to mourn with the weeping sisters and try to console them for the loss of their beloved brother. Jesus stopped at the wayside before entering the little town, and word of his approach soon reached the ears of Martha. As soon as she heard that Jesus was near she came running out to meet him.

"Lord!" she cried, as if with reproach. "If only you had been here, my brother would not have died." And then she added hastily, "But even now I know that, whatever you ask of God, he will give it to you."

"Your brother will rise again," Jesus comforted her.

"I know that he will rise again in the resurrection at the last day," said Martha sadly.

"*I* am the resurrection and the life," Jesus told her gently. "He who believes in me shall live, even though

he dies; and whoever lives and believes in me shall
never die. Do you believe that?"

"I do, Master!" said Martha. "I have believed and I
do believe that you are the Christ, the Son of God, who
was to come into the world."

And when she had said this she turned away and
went back to the house where her sister Mary sat and
mourned. She drew her sister aside and spoke to her in
secret.

"Mary," she said, "the Master is here, and he is
asking for you."

Mary sprang up quickly and ran out to meet him at
the place where he still waited, hoping to talk to him
alone. But the mourners who had been in the house
with her saw her leave, and supposed that she was going
to the tomb to weep. Therefore they followed her,
saying to each other sympathetically, "She is going to
the grave to wail and mourn."

But instead of coming to the tomb, they found themselves at the wayside watching the meeting between
Jesus and Mary.

Mary fell down at his feet and wept. "O, Master,"
she sobbed, "if you had only been here, my brother
would not have died." Now she was saying the same
thing as her sister had said, but she was expressing deep
faith rather than reproach; and a faith that was still
unchanged even though her brother had died. Martha
had not understood what Jesus had meant when he had
talked of resurrection, even though he had explained to
her. But Mary knew even without being told that Jesus
could still help them if he wished. The one thing she
could not know was whether or not it was the Father's
will that Lazarus might be saved.

In spite of her great faith, therefore, she sorrowed
and wept bitterly; and the Jews who had followed her
were weeping bitterly as well. Jesus himself was deeply
moved by their sorrow, and by the thought of the many
people of Israel who did not have Mary's faith and

would not rise again in the resurrection of the last day
to enjoy eternal life.

But the immediate problem was not one of eternal
life; it was the earthly death of a man who had believed
in God the Father and in Jesus as the Son. While Jesus
groaned within himself and his heart was troubled by
his thoughts, he was not so troubled that he could not
do what he had come to do.

"Where have you laid him?" he asked the weeping
woman.

"Come and see, Lord," Mary said.

She and the mourners led him to the grave. Martha,
watching from the house, saw the distant procession
straggling toward the burial place, and she stopped her
work to follow it.

Jesus still wept: wept for Mary and Martha in their
sorrow; for the grieving friends of Lazarus; for all those
who would not rise again. And the mourners saw his
tears.

"See how much he loved Lazarus," they whispered
to each other.

But others said, "Coud not this man, who has opened the eyes of the blind and done even more wonderful things, have prevented Lazarus from dying?"

Jesus again groaned within himself and walked up to
the tomb. It was a cave, and a heavy stone lay against it
for a door. Mourners crowded around; Martha hurried
from behind and joined them, wondering what Jesus
could possibly do now.

"Take away the stone," said Jesus.

"But Master!" Martha wailed. "He has been dead
four days. Already his body is decaying."

Jesus turned to her. "Did I not say to you that if you
would believe, you would see the glory of God?"

She nodded dumbly. Mary did not question him at
all, for her faith was strong. At a sign from her, the
mourners moved the great stone away.

Jesus lifted up his eyes to heaven and said: "Father, I
thank you for hearing me. I know that you do hear me

always, but I say this aloud to you now because of the
people who are standing here, so that they may believe
that you have sent me."

He lowered his eyes and looked into the open tomb.
"Lazarus, come forth!" he cried.

There was a quiet movement inside the cave. The
mourners watched, speechless with awe and something
close to fear.

A shadowy figure rose within the tomb. And Lazarus, who had been dead, came forth. His grave clothes
were still on him and his face was covered with a cloth;
but he moved, he walked.

Mary cried out with gratitude. The watchers gasped
and paled.

"Loose him," Jesus said. "Take off the burial
clothes, and let him go."

The grave clothes came off.

Lazarus was indeed alive; startled, but in perfect
health. The watchers rejoiced and fell to their knees in
reverence and thanksgiving. Martha and Mary wept
tears of joy, and took their beloved brother home
again.

Many of the Jews who had come to mourn Lazarus
came to believe in Jesus because of the remarkable
thing he had done before their very eyes. But some of
them went straight to the Pharisees, and told them what
they had seen.

The high priests and Pharisees at once called a meeting of the priestly council, a religious high court em-
powered to try any case involving Mosaic Law and
pronounce any sentence but that of death.

"What shall we do?" they moaned to each other.
"This man truly does many signs, or he seems to. If we
let him alone he will go on doing these things until all
men believe in him. And then the Romans will come
and take away both our holy place and our people. Yet
it seems that there is nothing we can do!"

Caiaphas, who was high priest that year, snorted
scornfully.

"You do not think at all!" he said sharply. "Nor do you consider that it is better that one man should die for the people than that the whole nation should perish on his account."

The Pharisees and priests were quick to see his point. So, from that day forth, they began to devise various plans for capturing Jesus and putting him to death.

Jesus knowing their purpose, walked openly among the Jews no more. He left Bethany, he left Judea; and he went with his disciples to a town called Ephraim in the country near the wilderness. Here they stayed until it was close to the time for another holy feast in the city of Jerusalem. Slowly they started to make their way back to the place which spelled so much danger for Jesus. The usual crowd followed and listened to all they said. There was much to talk about and much to do along the way, for time was running short.

They talked, first, of prayer, and Jesus told them a parable to show that they ought always to pray and never give up hope.

"There was once a judge," he began, "who neither loved God nor respected man. And in the same city there was a poor widow who had been wronged by an enemy. She went to see the judge, saying, 'Give me justice! Help me against that man.' But the judge brushed her aside. He had no interest in her troubles. The widow went to him again, and again, and then again; but he paid her no attention. Yet she kept going to see him and begging for justice, and after she had visited him many times the unjust judge said to himself: 'Why should I help her? I do not care for either God or man. But she keeps coming here to trouble me with her tale! I had better give her the justice she demands, or she will wear me out with her continual coming.' And so the judge did help her in the end.

"Learn from the story of this judge," said Jesus. "He did what the woman wanted because she came often to him. And shall not God, who is just and ready to listen, be much more willing to protect his chosen people when they cry to him by night and day? I tell you, he will do justice speedily! Pray often, therefore, and pray earnestly."

Now there were certain people in the crowd who were confident of their righteousness, and contemptuous of others whom they regarded as sinners. They were quite sure that they knew how to pray, even if no one else did.

To them, Jesus told this story:

"Two men went into the temple to pray. One was a Pharisee, and the other a tax collector. The Pharisee stood up boldly and prayed thus with himself: 'I thank you, God, that I am not like other men, the greedy and dishonest, the unjust, the adulterers, or like this tax collector here. I fast twice in the week, and I pay to the temple one-tenth of everything I get.'

"But the tax collector, standing at a distance, was so humble that he would not so much as lift his eyes to heaven. He stood with his head bowed and beat upon his breast, saying, 'God, be merciful to me, a sinner.'

"I tell you, it was this tax collector who went home with God's blessing, not the other. For everyone who exalts himself before God will be humbled, but he who humbles himself will be exalted."

A rich young ruler came to Jesus and asked what he might do to inherit eternal life. And when Jesus told him that he should sell his property and give his money to the poor so that he might have treasures in heaven, the young man went sorrowfully away. He could do anything but that, for he enjoyed his earthly wealth.

When he had gone Jesus said to his disciples, "Truly, I say to you, it is hard for a rich man to enter the kingdom of heaven." The twelve were amazed at these words, for, being poor themselves, they thought that the rich could do anything with greater ease than the needy. "Indeed," Jesus went on, "it is easier for a camel to go through a needle's eye than for a rich man to enter the kingdom of God. How hard it will be for those who trust in riches!"

"Who then can be saved, if not the rich?" his disciples asked.

"Those who truly believe," said Jesus. "The things which are impossible for men are possible with God, for with God all things are possible."

They were not far from the border of Judea when Jesus spoke again of his earthly destiny. He took his disciples aside, and as they walked along apart from the crowd he said to them:

"Behold, we go up to Jerusalem, and all things that are written by the prophets concerning the Son of man shall be accomplished. For he shall be betrayed into the hands of the chief priests and scribes, who will condemn him to death and deliver him to the Gentiles. And they will mock him, treat him shamefully, and spit on him. And then they will flog and crucify him; and on the third day he will rise again."

Even knowing this, he still turned his face toward Jerusalem.

# The Way to the Cross

\*\*\*\*\*\*\*\*\*\*\*\*\*\*\*\*\*\*\*\*\*\*\*\*

As they neared Jerusalem the disciples began to feel that they were on the eve of great events. They were sorely troubled by Jesus' words of death and resurrection, but they still supposed he meant the resurrection of the last day and that, therefore, the kingdom of God was immediately to appear. They still thought, too, that it would be much like an earthly kingdom, in which they would be offered positions of great power.

Yet they were wrong in this, and Jesus told them so with such bluntness that they became exceedingly disturbed by the prospect of entering Jerusalem. And they were right to be disturbed.

The Jewish passover was at hand, and many people had come up from the country to purify themselves before the festival. They looked for Jesus, and asked about him as they stood in the temple.

"What do you think?" they said to one another. "Do you think he will come to the festival? Or will he not, this time?"

For they knew that the chief priests and Pharisees had given orders that if anyone should find out where

Jesus was, he should announce it to them so that Jesus might be seized.

Six days before the passover Jesus went to Bethany to visit Lazarus and his sisters, and make his home with them until the day of the feast. On the day that he arrived, Simon, who had been a leper, made a supper for him in his own house. Lazarus sat near Jesus at the table, the practical Martha served, and Mary sought to find some way to show Jesus her love and trust.

She therefore brought in an alabaster flask containing a pound of liquid spikenard, a fragrant ointment that was exceedingly precious and costly. This she took to Jesus. First she anointed his head with the rare perfume. Then she knelt low in front of him, anointed his feet with it as if caring for a travel-worn visitor, and wiped his feet with her hair. It was a gesture of great love and gratitude, and of much deeper meaning than most of those present could understand. Some of the people at the table murmured indignantly among themselves, saying, "To what purpose is this waste of precious ointment?"

Judas Iscariot, the disciple who was in charge of their small treasury, spoke up sharply against Mary.

"Why was this ointment not sold for three hundred pence and given to the poor?" he demanded angrily. "Why should it have been wasted in this way?" Now he said this, not because he cared for the poor, but because he was a thief. He had charge of the money bag and he used every opportunity to take whatever was put into it.

"Let her alone," Jesus answered him. "Why do you trouble her? When she poured this ointment on my body, she did it to prepare me for burial. You will always have the poor with you, but you will not always have me. She has done a good deed. I say to you that wherever the gospel is preached throughout the world, this woman will be remembered, and what she has done will be spoken of in memorial to her."

Judas smarted under this gentle reproof. He was

already beginning to doubt that there would be any glory for him in the kingdom of which Jesus spoke, and he was interested above all in material things. So far he had gained nothing but some of the contents of the money bag. He fumed inwardly, and said no more.

Many of the people round about had heard that Jesus was at Simon's house, and they went there to see him, and not only to see him, but also to see Lazarus, who had been raised from the dead. They saw Jesus, they saw what Mary had done, and they saw Lazarus. And they were filled with wonder.

But the Pharisees, on hearing of all this, were driven to even further extremes of hate. Now they began to plot together so that they might also put Lazarus to death, because it was on his account that many of the Jews had come to believe in Jesus, and Judas Iscariot began to make certain plans of his own.

Meanwhile Jesus rested with his friends in Bethany on the sabbath day. Then he left them to go into Jerusalem. At Bethphage, near the Mount of Olives, he sent two of his disciples on ahead. "Go into the village yonder," he said. "As you enter it you will find an ass tied to a door, and next to it a colt that has never been ridden. Loose the colt and bring him to me. And if any man asks you, 'Why do you do this?' Tell him that the Lord has need of the colt and will send it back soon. Then the man will let you take the colt."

The two disciples went to the village and found the colt where Jesus had said it would be. As they were untying it, the owner came up and said, "Why are you loosing the colt?"

"The Lord has need of him," the disciples answered.

The owner nodded, as if he had been expecting this, and willingly let them go. The disciples then brought the colt to Jesus and made a simple saddle from their coats. And Jesus mounted the colt, sitting as comfortably as he could on his disciples' garments, and rode toward Jerusalem.

In doing so he was fulfilling the words of a prophet of old:

"Tell the daughter of Zion,
'Behold, your King comes to you,
Meek, and riding on an ass:
On a colt, the foal of an ass!' "

As Jesus approached Jerusalem with his disciples, pilgrims coming for the passover fell in behind. When the people of the city saw the procession coming toward them led by Jesus riding on the colt, great multitudes of them went out to meet him and lead him in. Some of them spread their garments across the road so that he might ride in greater comfort over the rough cobblestones; some cut palm branches from the trees and laid them across his path like a carpet for a king. As he drew near to the entrance of the city his disciples and the whole multitude began to rejoice and praise God for all the mighty works which they had seen.

"Hosanna!" they cried, waving palm branches and crowding around him as he rode. "Hosanna to the son of David! Blessed is the King of Israel, who comes in the name of the Lord! Blessed is the kingdom that comes! Peace in heaven, glory on high, Hosanna in the highest!" And the twelve disciples rejoiced at this tumultuous reception, and praised God in loud, exultant voices.

The Pharisees looked on helplessly. There was nothing they could do to Jesus while the crowds thronged about him and acclaimed him. But they did manage to draw close enough to speak to him of their displeasure.

"Rebuke your disciples!" they said harshly. "They should not cry out and say such things."

"No, I will not rebuke them," Jesus answered. "I tell you, if they should keep their silence, the very stones would cry out instead of them."

And then he rode into the heart of the city, all Jerusalem was stirred. People came out from their houses and asked each other, "Who is this?" and others answered: "This is the prophet, Jesus, from Nazareth of Galilee." For, even though it seemed that all Jerusalem was with him, and crying out: "Hosanna to the son of David!" there were few who truly believed that Jesus really was the Christ. Jesus knew that the day would come when they would suffer for their sins and unbelief; and he wept for them as he looked upon the city. After a brief visit to the temple he went back to Bethany.

On the following morning he returned to Jerusalem and entered into the temple of God, where once again he saw the money changers and sellers of sacrificial birds and beasts. And, as before, he cast out all those who bought and sold in God's house, driving away the sellers of doves and overturning the tables of the money changers. "It is written in the scriptures," he said to them, "that 'My house shall be called a house of prayer.' But you have made it a den of thieves!"

The sellers and the money changers went off in raging anger. But the blind and the lame came to Jesus in the temple, and he healed them.

The chief scribes and the Pharisees saw the wonderful things that he was doing, and they heard the children of the temple crying out joyously and saying, "Hosanna to the son of David!" Then they were even more indignant than before.

"Do you hear what these children are saying?" they said to Jesus angrily.

"Yes, I hear them," Jesus answered. "Did you never read, 'Out of the mouths of babes and sucklings you have drawn perfect praise'?"

When the priests and scribes heard this they decided that it was now time to destroy Jesus, for they feared that the multitude would cause such an uproar because of his presence that their Roman rulers would hear of it and be mightily displeased. Yet, because of that same multitude, they could find no way to do what they wanted: all the people seemed to be with Jesus, delighting in his teachings and hanging on his every word.

Therefore, because the Pharisees did not know what to do, Jesus was able to leave the city in safety and lodge once again in Bethany.

In the morning he came back to the temple, and the people came early to listen to his words. While he was teaching the people, the chief priests and the elders came to him and listened. Then they interrupted.

"By what authority do you do these things?" they demanded. "And who gave you this authority?"

But Jesus answered their questions with questions of his own which they could not answer, and they were silenced for a while. Yet still they watched him, and while they were not engaged in watching him they took counsel with each other as to how they might make use of his words to trap him and then turn him over to the ruling powers. They sent spies to him, Pharisees and men of Herod's party, who pretended to be honest men so that they might question him and twist his words. One unwise answer, and Jesus would be seized and handed over to Pilate, Roman governor of Judea. If the spies could only get him to say outright that he was King of the Jews, or persuade him to say anything against the Roman rulers, they would have him where they wanted him.

One of the spies approached Jesus with smiling face and honeyed words, and said: "Master, we know that you teach and speak the truth, regardless of what any man might think of you; and we know that you truly teach the way of God. Now tell us what you think: Is it lawful to pay the tribute tax to Caesar, or is it not?"

Now if Jesus said it was lawful, he would be admitting that Caesar was the rightful King of the Jews. And if he said it was not lawful, he would be saying something that the Romans could call treason.

But he saw their craftiness, and answered: "Why do you try to test me, you hypocrites? Show me the tribute money." They showed him a Roman coin called a denarius. Then he said to them, "Whose image is on this coin? Whose name is written on it?"

"Caesar's," they replied.

"Then give to Caesar what is Caesar's," Jesus said, "and give to God the things that belong to God."

They marveled at his answer. Their trick had failed, and so they went away to think of other traps. They hated everything he said: the things that they called blasphemy, and the things that they pretended to call treason. But the common people heard him gladly.

"Beware of the scribes," Jesus warned them even while the scribes themselves were listening. "Beware of the scribes and Pharisees who take widow's houses from them even while they make long prayers and pretend to be the most righteous of men. They shall receive the greater condemnation. They talk, but they do not act. They tie up heavy burdens and have them put upon men's shoulders, but they themselves will not lift a finger to move them. Everything they do, they do to be seen and praised by men: they love to have the chief seats in the synagogues and the chief places at feasts; they wear large tassels on their robes so that they will be admired, and the scripture texts they carry are twice as wide as those of anyone else; they desire deeply to be seen in long, flowing garments, and to be greeted with respect in the market places. Yet their long prayers are a pretense. All the things that they are seen to do are more important to them than prayers, for these things make them look important. But they are not important! I say to you that whoever exalts himself thus shall be humbled, and whoever shall humble himself shall be exalted."

He turned, then, from his friendly listeners to the others.

"Woe to you, scribes and Pharisees, hypocrites!" he said. "For you pay the tax of a tenth part of the herbs you gather and give it to the temple, thinking that you have thereby fulfilled your duties, but you leave undone the important matters of the Law—justice, mercy, and faith. Woe to you, you hyprocrites! You clean the outside of the cup and the platter, but inside they are full of your greed and evil-doing. You blind Pharisees! You must first clean the inside of the cup and the platter, so that the outside may also become clean. Be clean within yourselves, not only on the outside.

"Woe to you, scribes and Pharisees, hypocrites! For you are like whitewashed tombs: outwardly, they appear beautiful, but inwardly they are filled with dead men's bones and all uncleanness. In the same way you also appear outwardly righteous, but inwardly you are full of hypocrisy and sin.

"You serpents, you offspring of vipers! How do you think you will escape the judgment of hell? I will send you prophets, wise men, and scribes to help you. But some of them you will kill and crucify; and some of them you will flog in your synagogues, and persecute from city to city; and upon your heads will come all their righteous blood!"

And it was true that, in the years to come, the apostles of Jesus would be stoned and flogged and persecuted, and driven relentlessly from one city to another. Again, the masses, the common people, would welcome them as they now welcomed Jesus, but the rulers of the synagogues would not. And Jesus knew that these things would come to pass in later years.

When he had finished his outspoken condemnation of the scribes and Pharisees, Jesus began to mourn for a Jerusalem that would never really listen and believe. He knew that even among the crowds that professed to believe in him, there were relatively few people who believed with all their hearts and souls. Many would turn away from him before the end; many would lose their belief when he had gone. And the people of Jerusalem would suffer greatly for their sins.

"O Jerusalem, Jerusalem!" he cried, in an agony of pity for the holy city and its people. "You who kills prophets, and who stones those who are sent to you! How often have I wanted to gather your children together, even as a hen gathers her chickens, and you would not allow me! Behold, your house is left desolate. For I say to you, you shall not see me henceforth until you say, 'Blessed is he that comes in the name of the Lord.' "

No, they would never learn, least of all the proud men in positions of power and authority, no matter how boldly Jesus spoke or how many wonderful signs he showed to them. Indeed, at that moment, the scribes and Pharisees were almost speechless with wrath over the things Jesus had said to them and about them in front of the enthralled crowds in the temple.

# Last Hours
# in the Temple

✳✳✳✳✳✳✳✳✳✳✳✳✳✳✳✳✳✳✳✳✳✳✳✳

Jesus did not hesitate to reprove the self-righteous and the proud, even when they happened to be people in a position to do him great harm. At the same time he was quick to appreciate goodness of heart, and praise those who did well.

A short while after he had rebuked the scribes and Pharisees he sat down near the temple treasury and noticed how the people were casting money into it for offerings to God. Many who were rich were putting in large sums and making no attempt to conceal the generous size of their offerings. Jesus watched them with a feeling of sadness because of their pride. But then there came a poor widow who put in two tiny coins called mites, which together were less than a penny. And he felt glad because of her.

Even as she stood there, Jesus called to his disciples and told them what the woman had done. "Truly," he said, for all to hear, "I say to you that this poor widow has given more than anyone else who is casting money into the treasury. All the others are giving what they can easily spare from their abundance. But she, in need though she is, has put in everything she had. Out of her want and misery, she gave all her living."

Then he went again to teach within the temple, and great crowds gathered to hear him. Even Gentiles asked to see him, bringing requests that he might come to their own lands and teach them as he was trying now to teach the Jews. But he had already taught both Jews and Gentiles what he could in the short time that had been allowed to him. His fate now was to leave them all, and he would not change that even though he could.

Before he left the temple that day he said to those who were with him:

"The hour has come for the Son of man to be glorified. Truly, I say to you, that unless a grain of wheat falls to the ground and dies in bringing forth new wheat, then it remains but a single grain. But if it dies, it yields a great new harvest. For he who loves his life shall lose it, and he who gives up his life in this world shall have eternal life.

"If any man serves me, let him follow me. Wherever I am, there shall my servant be also. For if any man serves me, he will be honored by my Father."

Jesus paused, thinking of the pain and sorrow of the days to come.

"Now my soul is troubled," he went on at last. "And what shall I say? 'Father, save me from this hour'? No! it was for this very reason that I came; for this hour I came into the world. Father, glorify your name!" He bowed his head.

There came a voice out of heaven like a roll of thunder, and it said: "I have both glorified it, and I will glorify it again!"

The murmuring of the crowd became a sudden silence, and then again a stirring of hushed voices. Some who had heard the sound said that it had thundered. Others said, "An angel has spoken to him!"

"This voice did not come for my sake," Jesus said to them. "It came for your sakes, that you might hear and believe. This is a time of judgment for the world.

Through my death shall the prince of evil be cast out. And I, if I am lifted up from the ground, will draw all men to me." In saying this he was not only prophesying his own death to the multitude, but describing the manner of it, for he would indeed be lifted up from the ground to die. And in his death he would indeed draw men to him.

Voices from the crowd called out to him, saying: "We have learned from the Law that Christ shall endure forever. Therefore, if you are the Son of man, how can you say that you will be lifted up to die? Who, then, is this Son of man?"

Jesus did not answer them directly. "The light will be with you for only a little while longer," he said. "Walk while you still have the light, so that darkness may not overtake you, for he that walks in darkness does not know where he is going. Believe in the light while you have it, so that you may become the sons of light."

When he had said this he left the temple for the last time.

He and his disciples went together to the Mount of Olives. There they sat and talked, and Jesus told them that he would come to earth for a second time. And the day that he would come would be the last day of the earth, and all men would be judged according to their deeds.

"No man knows the day and the hour," Jesus said, "not even the angels of heaven. Only my Father knows. Watch, therefore, for you do not know when your Lord will come. If the master of the house had known what time the thief was coming, he would have been on watch and would not have allowed his house to be broken into. Be ready, therefore: do good, believe, and be prepared at all times for the coming of the Lord. Pray often, and be watchful of the things you do, for when the Lord comes he will expect you to have used the gifts he has given you, and used them well."

And he told a parable to illustrate his meaning.

"The coming of the kingdom of heaven may be

likened to a man who was going on a long journey. Before he left he called his bondservants to him and gave them charge of all his goods. And to one he gave five talents, to another, two, and to another, one, each according to the servant's ability. Then he went upon his journey.

"The man who had received the five talents immediately went and traded with them, and made another five talents. In the same way, the man who had received the two talents made another two. But the man who had received the single talent dug a hole in the earth and hid his master's money.

"Now after a long time the master of these servants came back and settled his accounts with them. The one who had received the five talents came and brought with him the other five talents he had earned. 'Lord,' he said, 'you gave to me five talents. See, I have made five more.'

"'Well done, my good and faithful servant,' his master said to him. 'You have been faithful over these few things, therefore I will set you over many things. Come, share with your master in his good fortune!'

"Then the one to whom he had given two talents came to him, saying, 'Master, you gave me two talents; I have gained two more.'

"His master said to him, 'Well done, my good and faithful servant. Come share with your master in his good fortune.'

"Then came the one who had buried his single talent in the ground.

"'Master,' he said, 'I knew that you were a hard man, demanding much from those who serve you. I was afraid of what might happen if I were to lose the talent, and I hid it in the earth. See, it is safe; I give it back to you.' And he gave the single talent back to his master.

"But his master was greatly displeased. 'You wicked and idle servant!' he said angrily. 'You say you knew that I was a hard man, demanding much of those who serve me. Then why did you not at least put my money into a bank? For then, at my return, I would have received it back with interest. But you have made nothing of it!'

"He turned to his other servants. 'Take the talent from this man and give it to the one who has ten talents,' he commanded. 'For everyone who has used what has been given him shall be given more in abundance, but he who has not used it shall lose even what he has. Now cast the unprofitable servant outside into the darkness, where he may weep and gnash his teeth.'

"Therefore, I say, be ready always; for the Son of man is returning at a time when you do not think it. Blessed is the servant who shall be found doing his duty when the Lord comes. And blessed is he who does his best with what he has been given, instead of simply making the least possible effort to fulfill his duty. He who works for his Master shall be well rewarded.

"And I tell you further how you shall be judged. When the Son of man comes in all his glory, and all his angels with him, he shall sit on his glorious throne; and all the people of the earth shall be gathered before him. Then the Son of man will separate them as a shepherd separates his sheep and goats, and some shall stand on his right hand and some on his left.

"To those on his right hand the King will say: 'Come, you whom my Father has blessed, enter now into the kingdom prepared for you. For when I was hungry, you gave me food. When I was thirsty, you gave me drink. When I was a stranger, you took me into your homes. When I was naked, you clothed me. When I was sick, you visited me. When I was in prison, you came to me.'

"Then all those who have been welcomed by the King will wonder, and say: 'Lord, when did we see you hungry, and feed you, or thirsty, and give you drink? When did we see you a stranger, and take you in? Or without clothing, and give it to you? When did we see you sick, or in prison, and come to you? We fed beggars at the door, and drew water for thirsty travelers; we gave to those in need, and we opened our homes to those who had no shelter; but never did we do these things for the Son of man.'

"And the King will answer: 'Truly, I say to you, you did these things for me. Whatever kindness you showed to anyone, even to the most humble of these my brothers, you have shown to me.' Then the King will say to those on his left hand: 'Depart from me, you accursed ones, into everlasting fire, for you did not try to help me.' And they will say to him, 'But we did not see you, Lord!'

"Then the Lord will answer, saying, 'You have not helped the least of my brothers. When you saw the hungry, the thirsty, or the strangers in need, you gave nothing to them; when there were those who were naked, sick, or in prison, you turned away and did not help them. And inasmuch as you failed to help the most humble of people, you failed also to do it for me.'

"Those on the left," Jesus said finally, "shall go away into eternal punishment. But those on the right, who were kind and righteous, shall have everlasting life."

When Jesus had told them these things about the day of judgment and the kingdom of heaven, he said to his disciples: "You know that after two days it will be the feast of the passover. That is the time when the Son of man will be betrayed, and afterward crucified."

Even as he spoke the chief priests and scribes and elders of the people were gathering in the house of Caiaphas, the high priest, to discuss how they might take Jesus by stealth and put him to death. They agreed that whatever they did must be done soon, before Jesus could leave Jerusalem again, and that it must be done with guile and subtlety so that he could not escape their clutches. "But it must not be done on the feast day," they said, "or there will be an uproar among the people."

They were still pondering the problem when one of the twelve disciples, he who was called Judas Iscariot, entered stealthily into the presence of the chief priests and offered them his services.

"What will you give me if I deliver him into your hands?" he asked them slyly. "For I can find a way to betray him to you."

They rejoiced when they heard his evil words, for to have help from within the ranks of Jesus' own disciples was an opportunity that could not be bettered. Therefore they gladly agreed to give the traitor thirty pieces of silver. Judas, in return, promised to turn Jesus over to them in such a way as to cause no trouble in the city.

And from that hour he sought a convenient moment at which to betray his Master. It would have to be a time when Jesus was not surrounded by the multitude, so that there would be no disturbance among the people to arouse the anger of the Roman rulers. And Judas thought he knew when that time might be.

# The Last Supper

*********************

Then came the first day of unleavened bread, the day on which the passover lamb must be sacrificed and eaten with bitter herbs.

The disciples came to Jesus, saying, "Where would you have us go to make preparations for the passover feast, so that we all may eat?"

Jesus chose Peter and John and instructed them to go into Jerusalem, for they still stayed in Bethany whenever Jesus was not teaching in the temple or talking to the twelve upon the Mount of Olives.

"When you have come into the city," he told them, "you will meet a man carrying a pitcher of water. Follow him into whatever house he enters, and say this to the man of the house: 'The Master says, "Where is my guest chamber, where I may eat the passover with my disciples?" ' Then he will show you a large upper room, furnished and ready, and there you will prepare for us."

Peter and John went into the city and found both the man and the house, as Jesus had said they would, and they made their preparations.

When evening came Jesus arrived and sat down with

the twelve. As they all took their places at the table, Jesus said to them: "How greatly have I wished to eat this passover with you before I suffer! For I tell you, I shall not eat another until it is fulfilled in the kingdom of God."

Then he took the wine cup, and when he had given thanks, he said:

"Take this, and divide it among yourselves. For I say to you, I will not drink again of the fruit of the vine until the kingdom of God shall come." He passed the wine cup around the table and all the men drank of it in turn like companions at a farewell supper.

As they sat there an argument arose among the twelve. As before, the dispute was concerned with which of them should be called the greatest in the coming kingdom. Jesus listened for some time. At last he spoke, saying, "Whoever is the greatest among you, let him be as the least. And he who is chief must be the servant of all."

Soon after he said this he arose from the table, laid aside his cloak, and fastened a towel about him. Then he poured water into a basin and began to wash his disciples' feet, wiping them with the towel that was about his waist. This was something that was usually done by servants at the beginning of a feast, but the disciples had no servants. And not one of them had thought to do this service, not even for their Master. Shame kept them silent until Jesus came to Simon Peter.

"Lord, Lord!" Peter protested. "Why do you wash my feet?"

"You do not understand now what I am doing," Jesus answered, "but you will understand hereafter."

"You shall never wash my feet," said Peter, and tried to pull away; for he did not want the Lord to do so humble a task for him.

"If I do not wash you, you have no share in my kingdom," Jesus said.

"Lord!" said Simon Peter. "Then wash not only my feet, but also my hands and my head!"

Jesus smiled gently. "Anyone who has already bathed needs only to have his feet washed to be wholly clean," he said. "You are already clean. But not all of you are clean." He said this because he knew that one of his disciples would betray him. And he knew which one it would be.

When Jesus had finished washing their feet he returned to his place at the table.

"Do you understand what I have done to you?" he asked. "You call me Master and Lord, and you say well, for so I am. If I then, your Lord and Master, have washed your feet, you ought also to wash one another's feet. For I have given you an example, so that you may also do what I have done to you and be my true disciples. Truly, I say to you: a servant is not greater than his lord, nor is he that is sent greater than he who has sent him. If you know and understand my commands, you will be blessed if you do them. But I know that you will not follow my example.

"I do not speak of all of you. I know whom I have chosen. But the scripture must be fulfilled that says:

" 'He who is eating bread with me
    Has raised his heel against me.' "

The disciples looked at one another doubtfully, wondering what he meant. Jesus himself was deeply troubled, for he loved his twelve disciples. Yet he knew that there was one among them who did not love him. He saw their wondering glances, and he sadly said: "Yes, it is one of you who will betray me; one of you who is eating with me at this very table."

Again they looked at each other back and forth across the table, feeling great sorrow in their hearts. Each man knew that he had weakness in himself, and each man feared that he might make some terrible mistake that would betray his Lord.

"Is it I, Lord?" each one said in turn. "Is it I?" And they began to question among themselves as to which one of them it was that would do this dreadful thing.

"Tell us who it is!" Simon Peter begged.

Jesus answered, "He that dips his hand with me in the dish, the same shall betray me." Now all of them had dipped in the same dish with him, so they still did not have the answer to their question. But then Jesus dipped a piece of bread into the dish in the middle of the table and handed it to Judas Iscariot.

"Is it I, Lord?" Judas whispered, so quietly that only Jesus could hear him.

Jesus nodded. "You have spoken. Whatever you do, do quickly."

No one but Jesus and Judas understood the meaning of this quiet exchange of words. The rest of the disciples thought that, since Judas held the money bag, Jesus had asked him to go out and buy extra things needed for the feast, or perhaps to give something to the poor. So they thought nothing of it when Judas, having received the piece of bread dipped in the bowl, left the room immediately and went out into the night.

There was no more talk of betrayal after Judas had gone, for as soon as he had left Jesus said to the rest of his disciples:

"My children, for only a little while longer shall I be with you. You will seek me when I have gone; but where I am going, you cannot come. I give to you now a new commandment: Love one another, as I have loved you. By this will all men know that you are my disciples—by your love for one another."

They continued with the meal, although all felt a heaviness of heart they had not known before.

It was almost over now.

Jesus took bread, blessed it, and broke it into small pieces.

"Take; eat," he said to his disciples. "This is my body, which is given for you. Do this in rememberance of me." They each took a piece, and ate.

And when the meal was over he took a cup of wine. He gave thanks and passed the cup to them. "Drink of it, all of you, for this is my blood and the new promise which I give to you. It is shed for you and for many, and it shall be poured out for many, for the forgiveness of their sins. Take it and share it among you. For I tell you again that I shall not drink of the vine until the day I drink it anew with you in my Father's kingdom."

They drank silently.

Then Simon Peter asked the question that had been troubling him.

"Lord, where are you going, that we may not come?"

"I have said to you that where I am going you cannot follow me now," said Jesus, "but you shall follow me afterward."

"But why cannot I follow you now?" asked Peter. "I will go anywhere; I will lay down my life for your sake. With you I am ready to go to prison and to death."

"Will you lay down your life for me?" said Jesus, in a voice of infinite sadness. "Truly I tell you, Peter, that before the cock crows tonight you will deny me three times."

"No, even if I die with you, I will not deny you!" Peter said vehemently. And all the other disciples, except for the missing Judas, said the same.

Jesus let it rest for the time being. Then he said:

"Let not your hearts be troubled. You believe in God; believe also in me. In my Father's house are many rooms. If it were not so, I would have told you. I go now to prepare a place for you. And if I go to prepare a place for you, I will come again to take you back with me, so that where I am, you may be also. You know the way to the place where I am going."

"But, Lord," Thomas said to him, "we do not know where you are going. How, then, can we know the way?"

"I am the way," said Jesus. "I am the way, the

truth, and the life. No one comes to the Father but through me, even as no one comes into the sheepfold but through me. And whoever has known me has known my Father also, for the Father is in me.

"And I go soon to my Father. Yet a little while here, and the world will see me no more. But I will not leave you desolate: the Holy Spirit shall be with you. And peace I leave with you; my peace I give to you, and not as the world gives it do I give it to you. Let not your heart be troubled, neither let it be afraid. You have heard me say that I am going away and coming back to you, yet you sorrow because I leave. But if you love me, you will be glad and rejoice, because I go to the Father and my Father is greater than I. I have told you all this before it comes to pass, so that you will believe me when it happens.

"I shall not talk much more with you. Arise, let us leave here."

And when they had sung a hymn, they went out into the Mount of Olives to find peace in the garden of Gethsemane.

Judas, in the meanwhile, was following their movements and reporting to the high priests and the elders.

As Jesus and his disciples went along their way in the darkness toward the garden, Jesus spoke another parable.

"I am the true vine," he said, "and my Father is the farmer of the vineyards. Every branch in me that does not bear fruit, he takes away. And every branch that does bear fruit, he prunes clean so that it will bring forth more fruit.

"Now you are the branches, and I am the vine. You are clean already, as the branches that have been pruned, because of the words which I have spoken to you. Abide with me in your hearts, and I shall abide with you. As the branch cannot bear fruit of itself unless it remains on the vine, neither can you bear fruit unless you abide with me in your hearts and I abide with you. He that abides with me, and I with him, will bear much fruit. But if your hearts are apart from me, you can do nothing.

"If you keep my commandments you will always keep my love, just as I have kept my Father's commandments and have always kept his love. This is my last commandment to you now: Love one another, as I have loved you. Greater love hath no man than this, to lay down his life for his friends. And you are my friends, if you do as I command you. No longer shall I call you servants, for the servant does not know what his master is doing. Now I call you friends, for all the things that I have heard from my Father I have made known to you.

"Until now you have asked for nothing in my name. But ask, from this time forth, and you shall receive so that your joy may be full. The Father himself loves you, because you have loved me, and have believed that I came from God.

"I say these things to you so that, through me, you may find peace. In the world you shall have tribulation. But be of good cheer, for I have overcome the world!"

Then Jesus raised his eyes to heaven. "Father! the hour is come," he said. "Glorify your Son, that your Son may also glorify you. You have given him power over all men on earth, that he should give eternal life to as many as you have given him. And this is life eternal: that they should know you as the only true God, and know that Jesus Christ is the one whom you have sent. I have glorified you on earth; I have finished the work which you gave me to do."

They came, then, to the brook Kidron, and there Jesus said to his eleven disciples: "All of you will forsake me this night. For it is written, 'I will smite the shepherd, and the sheep shall be scattered abroad.' But after I am raised to life I will go before you into Galilee."

Again, Simon Peter protested. "Even if they all desert you, I will not!" he swore.

And again Jesus answered, "I tell you truly, Peter,

that the cock shall not crow tonight until you have denied me three times over."

Then they crossed the brook and went together into the garden of Gethsemane. They all knew it well, for Jesus had often gone there with his disciples.

And Judas also knew the place.

# *The Betrayal*

As they entered the garden of Gethsemane Jesus drew three of his disciples to his side and said to the rest of them: "Sit here, while I go yonder and pray."

The eight men sat down beneath the trees at the entrance to the garden. Jesus took Peter, James, and John with him and walked along some little distance. And as he walked he began to think again of how he was being betrayed, of how he would be seized and beaten and led away to die. It would not be long now before the dreadful ordeal would begin. And at the thought of the betrayal and the suffering that was to come, Jesus' heart grew heavy and he was sorely troubled. He said to the three men with him, "My soul is exceedingly sorrowful, even unto death. Stay here, and keep watch over me while I am praying."

He walked on a little further into the grove of trees. Then he stopped, still in sight of the three on watch, and knelt to pray. "O my Father," he began, "if it yet may be, let this bitter cup pass away from me so that I do not have to drink of it. All things are possible for you; take from me this suffering, if you are willing. Nevertheless, let not my will, but yours, be done."

He prayed. But no sign came to him that he would be spared.

After praying for a time he rose up and walked slowly back to his three waiting disciples; and found them all asleep. He awakened them and said to Peter, "What, could you not watch with me one hour? Watch now, and pray that you do not fall into temptation. The spirit indeed is willing, but the flesh is weak. Sleep not."

He went away from them a second time and prayed, saying, "My Father, if this cup of suffering cannot pass me by without my drinking of it, then let your will be done."

Again he went back to his three disciples, and again he found them heavy-eyed with sleep. Nor did they know what to answer him when they awoke, even though he had so great a need for their love and support.

He left them and went away to pray a third time. In his agony of suffering and loneliness he prayed with even greater intensity than before, and the sweat rolled off his face to fall like great drops of blood upon the ground. Then there appeared to him a bright angel from heaven, to give him strength and comfort in his agony. Peace came into his heart. He rose, strong and ready for whatever was to come.

For the third time he went back to his disciples. "You may as well sleep on now, and take your rest," he said. "There is no longer any need to watch. Behold! the hour has come, and the Son of man is betrayed into the hands of sinners. He who betrays me is at hand."

And even before he had finished speaking there was a clamor of startled cries from the eight disciples at the entrance to the garden. Lights flickered through the trees and harsh voices gave commands. The sounds of clinking metal and heavy footfalls filled the night. And then the bright glow of lanterns and torches swept the grove and came to rest on Jesus.

In the gloom beyond the lights he could see a great band of soldiers, accompanied by officers from the chief priests and the Pharisees. The group came closer, and in the brightness that now was almost in their midst, Jesus and his disciples could see the clubs and swords carried by the intruders.

One man went slightly ahead of the group, leading the officers forward.

And then this one man, the betrayer of Jesus, gave a signal to the others, saying: "Whomsoever I kiss, that is he. Take him!"

Judas stepped forward and stood before Jesus with his arms outstretched in a gesture of false friendship.

"Hail, Master!" he said, and kissed Jesus on the cheek.

"Why have you come, my friend?" said Jesus. "Would you betray the Son of man with a kiss?"

The soldiers advanced upon him.

Jesus walked toward them. "For whom are you looking?" he asked.

"For Jesus of Nazareth," they answered.

"I am he," said Jesus calmly. They drew back, soldiers, priests and Pharisees, disconcerted by his manner.

He therefore asked again: "Whom do you seek?"

"Jesus of Nazareth," they repeated.

"I told you that I am he," said Jesus. "If it is I whom you seek, let these other men go their way without harm."

It was as if he himself had given a signal, for at these words the chief captain gave an order and the whole band rushed forward to lay rough hands upon him. For a moment there was a great confusion of clanking swords and milling men, even though Jesus stood there without moving, and in the turmoil Simon Peter drew a sword and slashed at one of the servants of the high priest. The blow struck savagely at the man's head and cut off his right ear. The man screamed with pain.

"Put up your sword!" said Jesus, already firmly bound with sturdy cords. "All who draw the sword shall die by it. Do you not know that I could beseech my Father to save me, and he would send more than twelve legions of angels to vanquish this band of men? But how then would the scriptures be fulfilled, which say this thing must happen?" Jesus turned then to the man whom Peter's sword had struck. "Let me first do this," he said. He touched the man's ear, and at once it was healed.

The soldiers clawed at Jesus, dragging him away. Chief priests, elders, and captains of the temple gathered around in triumph and shouted abuse while the armed men waved their weapons threateningly at a band of disciples who had no further thought of fighting back.

Then Jesus said to the ugly crowd:

"Do you come out with swords and staves to arrest me, as though I were a robber? I sat daily with you in the temple, teaching, and you did not stretch out a hand against me then. But this is your hour, the hour when the forces of darkness are in power. All this is happening now in fulfillment of the scriptures of the prophets."

The crowd fell upon him then to push and drag him from the peaceful garden to Jerusalem. And each and every one of Jesus' disciples turned, left their Master, and fled into the darkness. As for Judas, he had already gone his way.

The enemies of Jesus led him first to the house of Annas, father-in-law of Caiaphas the present high priest, and onetime high priest himself. He was still very influential among the priests and Pharisees, who deferred to his age and experience and often consulted him in cases involving serious breaches of Mosaic Law. Therefore, although their respect for him was hardly justified, they now brought Jesus to him for preliminary questioning.

Jesus stood in bonds before the old high priest. Annas heard the furious charges against him, and then began to question him about his disciples and his teachings.

Jesus told him nothing about his disciples. Nor would he say anything about his teachings. Instead, he said: "Why do you need to question me? I have spoken openly to the world. I have always taught in synagogues and in the temple, where all the Jews meet together and have heard me. I have said nothing in secret. Why, then, do you ask me? Ask those who heard me when I spoke; they know what I said."

One of the officers struck Jesus across the mouth. "Is that the way you answer the high priest?" the man said roughly.

"If I have said anything evil," Jesus answered calmly, "then say what evil I have spoken. But if what I have said is true, why do you strike me?"

Annas tried again. But he could get nothing out of Jesus that he could use as evidence against him. The old priest sent him, therefore, to Caiaphas the high priest, who had already called together certain chosen members of his council. They sat there waiting, the inner circle of priests, elders, and scribes, eager to see the Nazarene standing bound before them.

The officers brought Jesus into the council chamber.

And Simon Peter, who had fled with all the others, came back from hiding and followed at a distance as far as the court of the high priest. It was late by now, and chilly winds blew outside in the courtyard. Some of the servants and officers had built a fire to warm themselves against the chill of the night, and Peter went to share its warmth while he waited for the end of the scene within.

Inside, the chief priests and all the present members of the council sought false witnesses to offer evidence against Jesus so that they might put him to death. Many came forward, and many gave false statements, but none of the false statements agreed.

At last two false witnesses stood up confidently and declared:

"We have heard him say, 'I will destroy this temple

built by the hands of men, and in three days I will build another, which shall be made without hands.' "

But this was not what Jesus had said; and even the testimony of these two men did not agree.

Caiaphas the high priest stood up and faced Jesus. "Do you answer nothing?" he demanded. "What is this, that these witnesses say against you?"

But Jesus gave no answer. It was useless to explain what he had really said, or what he had meant by it. And in any event, what he had said would soon become a fact.

Caiaphas spoke again. "I demand that you tell us, on your oath by the living God, whether or not you are the Christ, the Son of God."

And Jesus said: "I am. And you will see the Son of man sitting on the right hand of the Almighty, and coming upon the clouds of heaven!"

The high priest tore his clothes with rage and triumph. "He has spoken blasphemy!" he cried. "What further need have we of witnesses? We ourselves have heard the blasphemy from his own mouth! What do you say now, you priests and elders?"

"He is worthy of death," some answered at once, and others took up the cry: "Yes, he deserves to die!" And they all condemned him to death.

Then some began to spit upon him and to strike him. Those who were holding him mocked him and beat him with their fists, saying, "Prophesy, you Christ!" Then they blindfolded him and struck him again with evil glee. "Show us that you are a prophet! See if you can tell us who it was who struck you!" And they all struck him and abused him without mercy.

The long night wore on and still they treated him unmercifully, shameful in their actions and shameless in their vindictive triumph. When it was almost dawn the chief priests, scribes and elders of the people, all the members of the council, held a final consultation over Jesus. It was formally decided by them now that he should be put to death. Yet they could not effect the sentence without first convincing the Roman procurator that it must be done.

Meanwhile, Peter was still waiting in the outer court, sitting there and warming himself by the fire in the cold first light of dawn. A maidservant at the courtyard door saw him where he sat. She looked at him searchingly. Surely, she thought, she had seen this man before. Of course she recognized him! She went to him and said: "You were with this Jesus of Nazareth. Are you not one of his disciples?"

Peter was suddenly filled with the fear he had felt earlier in the garden of Gethsemane. And all he could think of was the violent death that he might suffer if he admitted to being a follower of Jesus.

"No!" he said. "I do not know what you are saying." Nervously, he moved from the courtyard to the porch.

Shortly after that a second woman saw him. "This man is one of those who were with Jesus of Nazareth," she said to others who stood nearby; and she looked accusingly at Peter.

Again he denied it with an oath. "I do not know the man!" he said.

Next one of the servants of the high priest, a kinsman of the man whose ear Peter cut off, came up to him and stared him in the face. "You! You Galilaean!" he said. "You are one of them; I know you by your speech. And did I not see you in the garden with him when we came to seize him?"

"No!" said Peter. And he began to curse and swear. "I do not know the man; I do not know what you are talking about."

And immediately, the cock crowed in the blue light of the morning.

At that moment Jesus came out from the high priest's house, bound with tight cords and pushed rudely by the attendants of the priest. He turned and looked at Peter with compassion as he passed. Peter saw him and turned his eyes away. He remembered, now, those words of Jesus: "Before the cock crows, you will deny me three times."

And Peter had denied him thrice. He went out from the courtyard, weeping bitter tears.

# The Trial

✦✦✦✦✦✦✦✦✦✦✦✦✦✦✦✦✦✦✦✦✦✦✦

The death sentence had been passed by the council of the Jews, and now all that remained to be done was to obtain the official approval of their Roman ruler. A great company of people led Jesus to Pontius Pilate, procurator of Judea, for final judgment. High priests and chief Pharisees took up the lead. Behind them came the false witnesses who had spoken against him, various hirelings who had been persuaded to shout abuse against the man whom others called King of the Jews, and numbers of people who had little understanding of what was happening but had been attracted by the crowd. In the midst of all was Jesus, still bound and pushed along by soldiers who did not care what he had done but knew that he must not escape.

Pontius Pilate came out into the courtyard of his palace and stared at the multitude. There were high priests there, he saw, and elders of the people, and many others whom he did not know. In the midst of all there stood a man who clearly was their prisoner. The man's wrists were tightly tied together, his simple robe was soiled, and he had evidently been beaten without mercy. Yet he seemed serene and unafraid.

Early though it was, Pilate was ready to listen to their case. It must surely be important, or they would not have come at this hour, least of all with their high priests in the lead looking both outraged and triumphant.

"What accusation do you bring against this man?" asked Pilate.

"He is an evildoer," Caiaphas and Annas answered him, "or we would not have brought him to you. He has been corrupting our nation, forbidding people to give tribute to Caesar and saying that he is Christ, King of the Jews." Now in saying this they were not bringing up their own charge of blasphemy, for they knew that Pontius Pilate had no interest in their religious laws. But they were sure he would be interested in a Jew who claimed to be a king and refused the tribute to Caesar, for this was treason against the Roman rulers.

Yet they had not read Pilate as accurately as they thought. The Roman ruler caught the phrase, "King of the Jews," and decided at once this was a Jewish religious question and therefore none of his concern.

"Then try him yourselves," said Pilate, "and judge him according to your own Law."

"We have tried him," they answered. "But we have no authority to put any man to death."

Pilate knew that very well. But he had not expected them to ask the death sentence.

He looked again at the captive Jesus and saw a most unlikely looking king, and a most unlikely looking criminal. And as he looked the chief priests and the elders shouted accusations against the prisoner, accusing him of many things; yet the prisoner himself said nothing. Pilate found this very strange, for he had seen many prisoners before and they had always been vigorous in their own defense.

"Do you have no answer for them?" Pilate said to Jesus. "Do you not hear how many things they charge you with?"

But Jesus made no answer to any of the accusations.

He only stood there, dignified and calm; so calm that Pilate marveled greatly, turned away, and went back into his palace, for he knew nothing of this prisoner and realized he would find out nothing while the mob was screaming accusations in the courtyard.

From the judgment hall of his palace he there sent for Jesus.

Jesus came in and stood before him; still bound, still unafraid.

And Pilate the governor asked him: "Are you the King of the Jews?"

"Do you ask me this because you think it yourself?" said Jesus. "Or have others told you this about me?"

"Am *I* a Jew?" answered Pilate. "Your own people and the chief priests handed you over to me. What have you done? Do they accuse you rightly?" For he wanted to know if Jesus really claimed to be their king.

"My kingdom is not of this world," Jesus answered. "If it were, my men would have fought to keep me from being delivered into the hands of the Jews. No, my kingdom is not here on earth."

"Then you *are* a king?" said Pilate.

"You say rightly. I am a king," Jesus answered. "It was for this that I was born, and for this that I have come into the world: to testify to the truth. Everyone who is on the side of truth listens to my voice."

Pilate stared at him. "What is truth?" he asked.

With these words he arose and strode out into the courtyard once again to face the Jews. He had heard all he needed to hear: Jesus had said, "My kingdom is not of this world," and to Pilate that did not sound like treason against the Roman emperor.

"I find no fault in this man," he said.

The priests were thunderstruck that Pilate should have found Jesus innocent. Mutterings broke out in the crowd they had gathered to lend weight to their false cause, and the priests themselves became increasingly urgent in their demands.

"He is stirring up the people!" they cried fiercely. "He has been teaching his radical doctrines throughout all Judea, beginning in Galilee, going all over the countryside, even coming here to Jerusalem!"

"Oh?" said Pilate. "Galilee? Is this man a Galilaean?"

"Yes, he is from Nazareth."

"Ah." Pilate was glad to hear it. The whole affair was becoming a nuisance to him. If this Jesus was a Galilaean, he came under Herod's jurisdiction. And Herod could take care of his own.

So Pilate sent Jesus and his accusers to Herod Antipas, who also happened to be in Jerusalem at that time because of the festival.

Now when Herod saw Jesus he was exceedingly glad, for he had long been interested in seeing this man. He had lost his earlier desire to send out soldiers to seize him, for by all accounts the man Jesus was not John the Baptist risen again, nor had he spoken out against Herod as had John. Nevertheless, Herod had heard many extraordinary things about the Nazarene, and he was most anxious to see some miracle performed by him.

Therefore he greeted Jesus with enthusiasm, though without cordiality, and questioned him at length. But Jesus gave no answer to Herod's questions, nor any sign of his miraculous powers. Herod soon tired of him; this was poor sport indeed. He let the chief priests and scribes have their turn to speak. And they were only too willing. Vehemently they accused Jesus of inciting rebellion among the people, of refusing to pay tribute to Caesar, of claiming to be the Messiah, the King of the Jews. But Herod was not interested. He had only wanted to see signs, and he had seen none. Certainly h' could see no evidence of treason, and obviously the m; was no threat either to the Romans or to Herod h' self.

The only thing that caught the tetrarch's interes' that this quiet man before him could claim to '

King of Israel, or the King of the Jews. And that in it-self was Judea's problem, not Herod's. Still, it was an amusing thought and Herod smiled. A king, was he? And Herod laughed as he struck upon an idea that entertained him greatly. At least he would have some enjoyment from all this!

"Bring robes!" he ordered his palace guards. "If this man is a king, then let him look like a king!"

So they dressed Jesus mockingly in regal robes, laughing at their own cleverness, and they ridiculed him as he stood there in the finery they had forced upon him.

But soon they tired of this, too, for Jesus seemed untouched by their mockery; and they stopped their jeering and sent him back to Pilate.

Pilate was not pleased to see the Jews returning with their captive. He called together the chief priests and the leading members of the council, and all the people who had demanded that he pronounce sentence upon Jesus.

"You brought this man to me," he said, "as one who has misled the people with false claims. I have exam-ined him before you and have not found him guilty of any of the things of which you have accused him. Nei-ther has Herod found him guilty, for he sent him back to us. This man has done nothing to deserve death. I will therefore have him flogged, and then release him."

The crowd stirred restlessly. Flogging with the metal-tipped scourge was a terrible punishment, but it was not death. And they wanted Jesus dead. Certainly they did not want to have him released.

Now at the time of festival it was customary for the governor to release to the people any prisoner they chose; and at this particular time a notable prisoner named Barabbas was lying bound in a dungeon. Barab-bas was a revolutionary who had stirred rebellion among the people, in addition to being a robber and a murderer; and while Pilate himself definitely preferred to have such a man languishing in jail, the people themselves had no great interest in Barabbas either in prison or out, until Pilate now gave them a choice.

"Shall I then release the King of the Jews, in accordance with your custom?" Pilate asked. "Or whom would you have me release—Barabbas, or Jesus who is called the Christ?" He hoped that the crowd would call for Jesus, for he knew that the high priests had delivered Jesus to him out of envy and he did not wish to condemn the Nazarene to death.

But the mob gathered by the priests and Pharisees cried out together: "Not this man! Away with Jesus! Release not him, but Barabbas!"

Pilate was deeply disturbed by their answer. And while he sat there on the judgment seat, hesitating, he received a message from his wife. It said: "Have nothing to do with harming that good man, for I have suffered many things this day in a dream because of him." At this, Pilate was even more worried than before. He mulled the problem over in his mind. Even while he was doing so the chief priests and elders were arousing the multitude to cry out for Barabbas so that Jesus might be destroyed.

In spite of the rising tumult, Pilate asked again: "Which of the two would you have me release?"

"Barabbas! Barabbas!" they shouted back.

"Then what would you have me do to Jesus, who is called Christ?" Pilate asked them.

"Crucify him! Crucify him!" the people screamed.

"Why? What evil has he done?" asked Pilate. "I have found nothing in him to warrant his death. I will therefore chastise him and release him."

"No! Crucify him, crucify him!" screamed the crowd. "Give us Barabbas instead!"

But Pilate sent for his guard so that Jesus might be flogged, for he thought that, once the crowd saw the dreadful punishment inflicted upon Jesus, they would relent and no longer demand his death.

Pilate's soldiers flogged Jesus brutally. When they had done, they led him into the common hall and gathered about him with glee upon their faces. They stripped him of his tunic and dressed him in a purple robe such as a very great king might wear; and they wove a wreath of thorns and placed it on his head as if it were a crown; and they thrust a tall reed into his hand as if it were a scepter. Then they bowed low and knelt before him as though in worship of a mighty king.

"Hail, King of the Jews!" they mocked.

When they had had enough of this they took the sturdy reed and struck him with it, and they spat upon him. Then they led him back to Pilate.

Pilate once again went out into the courtyard and said to the waiting priests and multitude: "Behold! I bring him out to you, so that you may know that I find no fault in him." Surely now, he thought, the council and the people would have had enough.

Jesus came out wearing the crown of thorns and the purple robe.

Pilate pointed at him. Jesus was gaunt and bleeding, a travesty of a king in his mock-regal raiment; but still he stood upright and moved with quiet dignity.

"Behold the man!" said Pilate.

Whipped into yet greater frenzy by the high priests and their officers, the crowd cried out: "Crucify him! Crucify him!"

"Take him and crucify him yourselves, then," Pilate said, frightened by their ferocity. "I can find no crime in him."

But the Jews, under Roman law, were not permitted to execute a man themselves. The Romans had to do it for them. And it was clear to the high priests and the Pharisees that Pilate was still trying to avoid pronouncing an official sentence.

"We have a Law!" the Pharisees shouted. "And by our Law he deserves death for declaring himself to be the Son of God!" The crowd roared again, and this time there was a note of menace in their cries.

Pilate, hearing it, became even more afraid. He led

Jesus to one side and asked him, almost desperately, "What *are* you?"

But Jesus made no answer.

"Do you refuse to speak to me?" said Pilate. "Do you not know that it is within my power to release you, or have you crucified?"

"You have no power against me that is not given to you from above," Jesus answered. "The man who betrayed me to you has committed the greater sin."

At this, Pilate tried again to release him, but the Jews cried out: "If you free this man, you are no friend of Caesar's! Anyone who pretends to be a king commits treason against Caesar!"

"Then shall I crucify your king?" said Pilate.

"He is not our king!" the high priests shouted back. "We have no king but Caesar! Are you not Caesar's friend?"

By now their threat was obvious, and Pilate really was afraid. If what they were saying came to Caesar's ears, he himself would be in jeopardy. Already it looked as though a riot might develop, and this in itself would be enough to endanger his position.

He therefore sent for a bowl of water and washed his hands before the crowd. "I am innocent of the blood of this just man," he said. "You must see to it yourselves."

Then all the people answered, "Let his blood be on us, and upon our children!"

Pilate pronounced sentence. He released Barabbas to them, and he called his soldiers to give them their instructions. When they had finished mocking Jesus in his purple robe, they took it off and dressed him once again in his own simple garment. Then, leaving the crown of thorns upon his head, they led him away from the governor's palace to be crucified.

And Pilate, having washed his hands of the whole affair, left them to it.

Now Judas Iscariot, the betrayer of Jesus, was hovering on the fringes of the crowd as it neared the city gate, and soon discovered that Jesus had been condemned to death by crucifixion. Suddenly he was stricken with terrible remorse for the treacherous thing he had done. With a greatly troubled heart he went back to the chief priests and elders with his thirty pieces of silver.

"I have sinned!" he said. "I have betrayed an innocent man."

They looked at him with scorn. "What is that to us?" they said. "That is your affair; answer for your own sin."

In an agony of repentance the traitor threw the pieces of silver on the temple floor. Then he ran out of the temple to a lonely place outside the city.

The chief priests picked up the pieces of silver. At this moment even they felt some slight sense of shame. "It is not lawful for us to put this money into the treasury," they said, "because it is the price of blood."

They therefore took counsel with each other, and after some discussion they decided to use the money to buy the potter's field for the burial of penniless strangers. The ground they afterward purchased with the blood money has been called the Field of Blood to this very day. And because it was a potter's field, any piece of ground used as a graveyard for unknown persons or the very poor is still, today, known as a potter's field.

The crowds, with Jesus in their midst, milled through the northern city gate.

And Judas, in the lonely place, hanged himself upon a tree.

# The Crucifixion

✚✚✚✚✚✚✚✚✚✚✚✚✚✚✚✚✚✚✚✚✚✚✚

It was still early on that long morning of trial and condemnation when Jesus started his last and most painful journey.

The Roman soldiers led him through the north gate of the city to the place of death, called Calvary by the Romans and known as Golgotha in the Hebrew tongue. Both names mean "The Place of the Skull." Jesus staggered up the hillside carrying the heavy cross upon which he was later to be nailed, for it was the custom among the Romans that those who were about to die by execution should carry their own crosses.

His back was bowed beneath the weight of the great wooden beam as he walked, and his feet stumbled on the rough road. A great company of people gathered and followed him as he slowly climbed the hill to Calvary. Some were enemies who mocked him, some were passing strangers who joined the throng through curiosity or chance, and some were his friends who longed to help him but could not. The women among them wailed and wept, lamenting Jesus and beating their breasts with sorrow as they saw his suffering and knew that worse was yet to come.

And even with the racking pain in his body and the cross upon his back, Jesus saw their sorrow. He turned his head to them and said: "Daughters of Jerusalem, do not weep for me. Weep rather for yourselves and for your children, for a time is coming when it will be said, 'Happy are the childless, who have no little ones to be slain, and happy are those who never will have children.' For when Jerusalem suffers for its sins it will be well for those who have no young ones, for not even the youngest will be spared. And at that time the people of the city will say to the mountains, 'Fall on us!' and to the hills they will cry, 'Cover us!' so that they might escape their fate. But there will be no escape, for if this is what they do when I am here, what will they do when I am gone?"

He stumbled on beneath the cross, carrying it upon his wounded shoulders. But he had been so badly beaten that his strength was almost gone, and at last he fell and could not rise. The soldiers cursed and prodded him. But still he could not manage to struggle to his feet with the weight upon his back.

"You, there!" the soldiers shouted, and they seized upon a man in the crowd who knew nothing of what was happening. The man was Simon of Cyrene, who was coming in from the country; and they laid the cross upon his back and compelled him to carry it after Jesus. Jesus therefore rose and walked on slowly.

The procession continued. Now two other doomed men, common criminals, were brought into it to be led with Jesus to the place of death.

At last they all reached the Place of the Skull. When they came to the hilltop the soldiers ordered Simon of Cyrene to lay the cross down flat upon the ground. Then they removed Jesus' clothes and made him lie upon the cross. They nailed him to it through his hands and feet. Now they raised the cross and planted it firmly in the earth. Meanwhile, other guards were preparing the two criminals for crucifixion, and when the three crosses were raised Jesus was in the center with one robber on his right hand and the other on his left.

The soldiers offered Jesus a drink of sour wine mixed with bitter gall, but he refused it. And as he hung there on the cross awaiting death, Jesus called out: "Father, forgive them, for they know not what they do."

There was little to do but wait. While they waited, the soldiers divided up the clothes that Jesus had been wearing into four parts, one for each man guarding him while he slowly died. But when they came to the tunic and saw that, instead of having a seam, it was woven in one piece from top to bottom, they decided that it could not be divided. Therefore they said to one another, "Let us not tear it, but cast lots among us to see who shall have it." They did so, and in doing it they fulfilled the psalm in the scriptures which read: "They divided my garments among them, and for my clothing they cast lots." All these things the Roman soldiers did, without knowing that what they were doing had been predicted centuries before.

Now Pilate had written a sign in letters of Hebrew, Latin, and Greek, saying: "THIS IS JESUS THE KING OF THE JEWS." When the soldiers had finished their business of dividing up the clothes they set the sign over Jesus' head and settled back to watch him die.

The people stood there staring at him. Others, passing by along the road, stopped to jeer at him and shake their heads in scorn.

"You who would destroy the temple and build it up again in three days, save yourself!" they mocked. "If you are the Son of God, save yourself and come down from the cross." The chief priests, with the scribes and elders, mocked him in the same way, saying: "He saved others, so we hear, but he cannot save himself. He is the Christ, the King of Israel and the chosen one of God! Therefore let him now come down from the cross, and we will believe in him. He trusted in God;

let God now deliver him if he wants to. For this man said, 'I am the Son of God.' "

But though Jesus could have come down from the cross he would not, for death on the cross was his destiny.

The soldiers mocked him, too. They came to him offering him sour wine to moisten his dry lips, and said: "If you are the King of the Jews, let us see you save yourself!"

Even the robbers who were being crucified alongside him abused him. One in particular mocked and cursed at Jesus. "Are you not the Christ?" he said. "If you are, save yourself and us!"

But as the time passed and the first man received no answer, the second man began to see in Jesus a quiet strength he had not seen before. He therefore rebuked the other, saying, "Have you no fear even of God, when you are suffering the same penalty as this man? We two are suffering justly, for we deserve to die for what we have done, but this man has done nothing wrong." Then he turned his head to look at Jesus. "Lord," he said, "remember me when you come into your kingdom, for I believe in you."

And Jesus answered him, saying, "I tell you truly, today you will be with me in Paradise."

Then he looked down to see those who stood near him. Close to the cross stood his mother, his mother's sister, and Mary Magdalene, and only one of his disciples. Both Lazarus, whom he had raised from the dead, and the eleven men who had been his most devoted followers, were still in danger from the vengeful priests and Pharisees. Most of them, therefore, were afraid to be seen near him even while he was dying on the cross. But John at least, whom Jesus dearly loved, was there with the wailing women.

When Jesus saw John standing at his mother Mary's side and trying to comfort her, he called down from the cross. To his mother he said: "Woman, behold your son John!" And to John he said: "John, behold your mother! Care for her." And from that hour John took Mary into his own home and cared for her as if she were his mother.

The painful hours dragged by. High noon came, and the sun blazed overhead. Then suddenly the sun was covered by black clouds, and darkness fell over all the land. A strong wind swept the hill upon which the crosses stood, an eerie sound in the strange darkness of the day. Many of the people shook with fear and many of them left the place of death, trying to escape their fear. But many others, friends and enemies alike, stayed to see the end.

Three hours later, under a sky still ominously dark, Jesus cried out suddenly: "My God, my God, why have you forsaken me?" His hearers recognized the words, for they were also in the scriptures that had foretold the manner of his death. There was a brief silence, and the sky began to brighten.

Then Jesus spoke again, once more fulfilling the scriptures.

"I thirst," he said.

There was a bowl of the sour wine standing by. One of the watchers took a sponge and soaked it in the wine, then put it on a reed and held it up so that Jesus might drink. And some of the others jeered, saying: "Let us see whether Elijah comes to save him!"

Jesus moistened his lips with the sour wine. His work was now accomplished and he was ready to free his spirit. He cried out again in a firm, clear voice:

"It is finished!"

And to his listeners it sounded not like a cry of despair, but a cry of victory.

Now Jesus spoke his last words on the cross. "Father, into your hands I entrust my spirit."

When he had said this, he bowed his head, and died.

At the very moment in which he yielded up his spirit the curtain that veiled the inner sanctuary of the temple in Jerusalem was torn in two from top to bottom. The earth quaked, great rocks shattered; tombs opened, and saints rose from their sleep to leave their graves.

The Roman centurion in charge of the guard saw how Jesus had yielded up his spirit; he saw the earthquake and many other strange and wonderful things that happened in the moment of Jesus' death, and he was so frightened and amazed that he cried out in glory of God. "This surely was a righteous man!" he said in awe. "Truly he must have been a Son of God!" And others echoed him.

But now it was all over. The crowds that had gathered to watch the spectacle turned away, beating their breasts, and went back to the city. But the friends of Jesus, and his mother, and many women who had followed him from Galilee, stayed there watching from a distance. Among them were Mary Magdalene, and Salome the wife of Zebedee and mother of James and John, and Mary the wife of Alphaeus and mother of the other James. All had loved him deeply; and all were overcome with sorrow for their Master and for his weeping mother.

It was now mid-afternoon, and the beginning of the sabbath would come with the setting of the sun. And because the bodies could neither be removed from the crosses or allowed to remain upon them on the sabbath day, least of all during the passover season, the Jews went to Pilate and asked that the bodies be removed at once. Pilate agreed to their request and sent his soldiers back to Calvary.

First they made sure that the two robbers were dead. Then they came to Jesus. They knew he was already dead, yet one of the soldiers thrust a spear into his side; and from the wound there flowed both water and blood. They stared at the limp body in surprise, not knowing that they were fulfilling yet another prophecy: "They shall look upon the man whom they have pierced."

When it was close to evening there came a rich man from Arimathea, named Joseph, who went to see Pilate to ask for the body of Jesus. Now Joseph was a Pharisee and a respected member of the council, but like Nicodemus he was a good and righteous man who had vehemently objected to any suggestion that Jesus might be harmed. In fact, when the council had held their hasty pre-dawn meeting, they had taken good care to exclude both Joseph and Nicodemus. They knew that these two men were sympathetic toward the Nazarene. What they did not know was that both of them were actually disciples of Jesus, and were themselves looking for the kingdom of God through the man from Nazareth.

And now Joseph of Arimathea stood boldly before Pilate, asking for the body of Jesus so that he might bury it. Pilate granted permission.

Joseph therefore went to the place of death, taking with him fine linen cloths to wrap around the body. Nicodemus went also, taking a mixture of myrrh and aloes to perfume the grave clothes. Ordinarily the body would be carefully washed and anointed before burial, but there was no time for that. Together the two men took Jesus down from the cross. Together they bound his body in the linen cloths with the spices, in accordance with the Jewish custom. Then, with the help of friends, they gently carried Jesus to a tomb in a garden near the place of the cross.

It was Joseph's own new tomb, one that he had hewn from rock for the day of his own burial, and no man had ever yet been laid in it. Now Joseph was using it as a resting place for Jesus so that the Master might be buried before sundown, and in a place where his body would be safe from enemies who might wish to steal or desecrate it.

The eleven disciples were hiding in Jerusalem. But the women who had come from Galilee followed the small procession and saw Jesus being gently placed within the tomb. Then Joseph rolled a great stone against the mouth of the tomb and departed for his home. When this was done the women left, too, and went off, mourning bitterly. And they rested on the sabbath day, according to the commandment.

The first night of sorrow passed. Very early in the morning the chief priests and Pharisees hurried off to Pilate and made another request. For during the night they had been struck by a thought that had not even occurred to any of the followers of Jesus.

"Sir," they said to Pilate, "we remember that when the deceiver Jesus was alive he said, 'In three days I will rise again.' We ask, therefore, that you give orders to have the tomb closely guarded and secured until the third day. For it may be that his disciples will try to come at night and steal him away, afterwards saying to the people that he has risen from the dead."

"Take the guard." said Pilate. "Make the tomb as secure as you can."

So they went off with the officers and made the grave as secure as they could by sealing the stone and leaving a guard on watch.

This was the second day of Jesus' death.

When the sabbath was over at sunset of that day, Mary Magdalene and Mary the mother of James, and Salome who had followed Jesus through Galilee, went out and bought sweet spices and ointments so that they might properly anoint the body of Jesus whom they loved. When the night had passed and the early morning hours had come, they would go to the tomb and make the burial preparations for which there had been no time before. So the women made plans to go to the garden first thing in the morning.

But the eleven disciples remained behind closed doors, afraid for themselves and full of sorrow over Jesus. They had wanted a king and they had dreamed of glory, and now the dream was gone with the death of Jesus. They had loved him; they had learned much from him; but they had never really understood all he had told them about the nature of the kingdom of God, or what he had meant when he said that he would rise again. Now they sat there without hope, staring silently at each other and not even thinking to count the days.

The morning of the first day of the new week dawned. It was the third day of the death of Jesus. The Roman soldiers still stood on watch outside the tomb. With the coming of the dawn the ground began to tremble and shake, and a great earthquake racked the garden where Joseph of Arimathea had laid Jesus in the cave. An angel of the Lord came down from heaven and rolled away the stone from the mouth of the tomb, and calmly sat upon it. His face was as bright as lightning, and his raiment as white as dazzling snow; and his watchers gaped and turned pale with fear. They stared at the angel, quaking, and so overcome with shock were they that they fell to the ground like men who had been struck dead.

When they recovered themselves they got up and fled into the city to report what they had seen. They ran very quickly, and they did not look back.

It was very early when Mary Magdalene and the other women came with their spices to anoint their beloved Jesus. The guard had gone, but this did not surprise them for they had not known that any soldiers had been posted. As they walked into the garden they were saying to one another, "Who will roll back for us the stone from the doorway of the tomb?," for the stone was much too heavy for the women to handle alone. Then they reached the tomb. And what they saw then did surprise them.

The stone had already been rolled back from the cave. And when they looked in through the open doorway they saw that the body of Jesus was no longer there.

# He Is Risen!

✛✛✛✛✛✛✛✛✛✛✛✛✛✛✛✛✛✛✛✛✛✛

The women stared amazed into the tomb. They could scarcely believe their eyes, for they had seen Joseph laying Jesus in the tomb. But it was true: Jesus was not there.

Mary Magdalene gasped with shock and fear. Her only thought was that the enemies of Jesus had come and taken him away from the place where he had been so lovingly laid. In her misery she turned abruptly and ran back into the city to find John and Simon Peter.

"They have taken the Lord away from the tomb," she gasped, "and we do not know where they have laid him!"

They were disturbed and puzzled. Not knowing what to do, they did nothing. Mary left them and wandered slowly back toward the garden.

Meanwhile, the Roman guards who had run from the tomb had gone straight to the priests to tell them what they had seen. They knew nothing of the visit of the women, but they did know that the body of Jesus was gone. The priests were angry and alarmed, although they could not blame the soldiers. After a quick consultation with the elders they decided on a course of action: they would lie. They gave the soldiers a large sum of money to hide the truth and tell a different version of their story.

"We will not have it said that Jesus is risen," they announced. "Tell people that his disciples came in the night and stole away his body while you slept. If news of this comes to Pontius Pilate and he accuses you of failing in your duty, we will persuade him that you were not to blame and see that no trouble comes to you." The soldiers therefore took the money and began to spread the false story among the people. And those who heard, believed them.

Now the other women who had been with Mary Magdalene were still within the tomb. But while they looked about it they saw that they were not alone. Jesus had indeed gone, but now they saw a young man in dazzling white apparel sitting at the right. There was a glow about him that amazed and frightened them.

"Do not be afraid," the angel said. "I know you are looking for Jesus of Nazareth, who has been crucified. He is not here, for he has risen. Remember, he said that he would be crucified and on the third day rise again." Then they did remember, and their hearts rose joyfully.

"See," said the angel, "here is the place where he was laid."

The women looked again, and saw the linen cloths that had been wrapped about his body. If they had thought, like Mary, that his body had been stolen, they saw now that it could not be so.

"Go quickly now!" the angel said to them. "Tell Peter and the rest of the disciples that he is risen, and say to them: 'He is going before you into Galilee, and you will see him there just as he told you.' "

The women hurried off, still awed and frightened yet overjoyed. They went at once to the place where Peter and the rest of the disciples were waiting for they knew not what. "He is risen!" the women said. The men stared blankly at them. Women! First Mary Magdalene, and now the rest of them.

But the women went on with their story. All they had seen and heard they told to the eleven disciples. And to the men their excited words seemed only to be idle tales, and they did not believe what they were hearing.

Yet when the women were gone Peter thought about their words. He rose, then, and ran quickly to the tomb with John. They stooped and looked inside. There was no body; neither was there a young man in shining white. There were only the linen grave clothes, and the face handkerchief neatly rolled up in a place by itself. This was not the work of vandals. But what was it? The two disciples turned and left, full of wonderment yet still without understanding of what had come to pass.

Now Mary Magdalene came walking through the garden, unseen by them and not seeing them herself. She stopped outside the tomb and quietly wept. And as she wept she, too, stooped and looked into the cave, for even through her tears she could see a bright glow coming from it. Inside she saw two angels dressed in dazzling white, one sitting at the head and one at the feet of the place where the body of Jesus had lain.

They said to her, "Woman, why are you weeping?"

"Because they have taken away my Lord," she answered sorrowfully, "and I do not know where they have put him."

When she had said this she turned away, too grief-stricken to realize that she had been talking to no ordinary men. Through her tears she saw a figure standing outside the tomb. It was Jesus, but she did not know that it was he.

"Why do you weep?" asked Jesus gently. "For whom are you looking?"

Mary looked at him through misted eyes and still did not know who he was. Supposing him to be the gardener who cared for Joseph's garden, she said to him: "Sir, if you have taken him away, tell me where you have laid his body, so that I myself may take him and place him somewhere else."

Jesus looked at her with love and said: "Mary!"

She turned and saw him anew. Now she knew the voice; now she knew the face. It was like the face of Jesus, and at the same time strangely unlike; and yet she knew that this was he.

"Master!" she cried. Full of joy and gladness, she reached her arms toward him in a gesture of worship and devotion.

"No, do not touch me yet," Jesus said in kindly tones, "for I am not yet ascended to my Father. But go to my brothers, to my friends, and tell them that I will soon ascend to my Father and your Father, to my God and yours. And I will see them before then."

As Mary looked upon him, he was gone.

She went at once to see the disciples to tell them that she had seen the Lord, and found them mourning and weeping still. She said that he was alive; she told them the things he had said. But they, sorrowing for his death and puzzled by the disappearance of his body, could not believe that he really was alive and that she had seen him. It was a woman's dream, they thought: she had wanted it to be true, and so she had believed. But they could not believe.

Now it happened that same day that two of Jesus' followers had left Jerusalem after the sad passover and were traveling along the road to Emmaus, a village about seven miles from the city. As they walked they talked sadly together about all the strange and terrible things that had happened. They had heard that Jesus had risen from the dead, but they did not believe what they had heard. All their bright hopes of a Messiah who would save Israel had been cruelly shattered, and only despair and misery were left.

While they walked, Jesus drew near to them in the form of a stranger, and they did not know him.

"What is it that you are discussing so earnestly as

you walk?" asked Jesus. "And why are you so sorrow-ful?"

They stopped and stood on the road, looking sad.

One of them, whose name was Cleopas, answered him, saying: "Are you a stranger in Jerusalem? You must be, for surely you are the only man in the city who does not know the things that have been happening here these last few days!"

"What things?" asked Jesus.

And they answered, "Why, the things concerning Jesus the Nazarene, who was a prophet mighty in deed and in word in the eyes of God and all the people. The chief priests and our rulers delivered him up to be condemned to death, and the Romans crucified him. We had hoped, and we believed, that he was the Christ who would be the Savior of Israel, but now he is dead. Besides all this, it is now three days since these things came to pass, and certain women of our company have astounded us. They went early to the tomb this morning but they did not find his body where it had been placed. No, they came back saying that they had had a vision of angels who had told them he was alive. Therefore some of us went to the tomb to prove what they were saying. We found it empty, as the women had said, but nowhere did we see our Lord."

"Ah, you are foolish," Jesus said. "And how slow of heart you are to believe all that the prophets have said! If you had believed, you would have known that all these things were to happen. Do you not remember that the Christ would have to suffer all these things before entering into his glory?" And then, beginning with the books of Moses, and going on to all the prophets, he interpreted for them all the passages in the scriptures that concerned himself. They listened eagerly, and much was made clear to them that they had not under-stood before.

When they drew near to Emmaus, where the two men lived, Jesus bade them farewell and would have gone on further. But the two men urged him not to go.

"Stay with us," they begged him warmly, "for it is getting toward evening and the day is almost over."

He thanked them and accepted.

They went into the house together and sat down to dine. Jesus took the bread and blessed it; then he broke it, and gave it to the other two. And all at once their eyes were opened, and they knew him. As they gazed at him in startled recognition, he vanished from their sight.

Then they rejoiced within themselves as they realized that their hopes of a redeemer had not been dashed, but had come true. He was alive! With great excitement they said to one another, "Were not our hearts glowing within us while he spoke to us along the way and explained the scriptures to us? We should have known then that he was the Christ!"

They rose that very hour and hurried back to Jerusalem, to the house in which the eleven disciples were accustomed to gather together. They were all there but one, and they welcomed the newcomers mournfully and firmly locked the door for fear of the Pharisees. The two men told the others everything they had seen and heard that day.

"The Lord is risen indeed!" they said. "We have seen him for ourselves." And they explained what had happened on the road, and how the stranger had come with them to their house to eat with them, and how they suddenly came to know him with the breaking of the bread.

As soon as they had finished their story, Jesus himself suddenly appeared in their midst and said to all: "Peace be with you!"

But his disciples felt by no means at peace. They were startled and terrified by this sudden apparition, for the door had been securely bolted in case of a surprise visit by any of their enemies, and they had been quite certain that no one could possibly get in. This sudden visitor must surely be a spirit! And they trembled with fear.

"Why are you so troubled?" Jesus asked. "And why are doubts and questions arising in your hearts? I am no ghost. See my hands and feet! It is I, myself. Touch me yourselves and see; feel me and find out that I am real. A spirit does not have flesh and bones, as you can see I have." And as he said this he showed them his wounded hands and feet, and his side where the soldier's sword had pierced him.

They believed and yet at the same time did not quite believe, for it was too wonderful to be true. They gazed incredulously at his living body and the deep, dark scars, amazed at what they saw. But he had died, they knew; this could not be he!

And while they wondered still, disbelieving through sheer joy, Jesus said to them: "Have you anything here to eat?"

One of them managed to pull himself together to find food. Jesus sat down at the table and they brought him broiled fish and a piece of honeycomb. He took the food and ate before their staring eyes. They watched as though they had never before seen a man at dinner. Yet when they saw him eat they knew he was indeed no spirit but a man; that he was Jesus, in the living flesh.

Then he said to them again, "Peace be with you! Now you see that all things concerning me, that were written in the Law of Moses, in the books of the prophets, and in the psalms, have been fulfilled." Then he opened up their minds so that they might more fully understand the scriptures, and he said to them: "It is written that the Christ should suffer, and rise again from death on the third day; and that repentance and the forgiveness of sins must be preached in his name to all the nations, beginning in Jerusalem. As my Father sent me, so will I send you."

And when he had said this he breathed on them and said: "Receive the Holy Spirit: if you forgive the sins of any man, those sins will truly be forgiven. And if you do not release any man from his guilt, the sins of that man will be retained."

They listened now as they had listened to him in the years before his death, and they knew for certain that he was Christ returned to them.

He left them, then, and they rejoiced that he had risen and come back into their midst.

But Thomas the Twin, one of the eleven, had not been with them when Jesus came. When he joined the others they told him at once and with great joy: "We have seen the Lord!" Thomas was a doubter; he still would not believe. He said to them, "Unless I see for myself the marks of the nails in his hands, I will not believe; and until I put my finger into the marks and my hand into his side, I will not believe." And there was nothing they could do to convince him that Jesus was alive.

Eight days later the disciples were again together in the house with the door firmly closed and locked. This time doubting Thomas was with them. Jesus appeared as suddenly as before and stood there in their midst.

"Peace be with you!" he said. And Thomas still looked doubtful.

"Thomas," said Jesus. "Come to me." Thomas went to him.

"Reach out your finger," Jesus said. "Look at my hands and touch the marks." Thomas did so. The expression on his face began to change. "Now," Jesus told him, "place your hand into my side." Thomas felt the wound. "Have faith; believe!" said Jesus.

"My Lord and my God!" said Thomas then. "I do believe." And he was filled with joy.

Jesus said to him, "Only because you have seen me, do you believe. But blessed are those who have not seen me, and even so, believe."

Now all eleven of them knew that Jesus had indeed risen from the dead as was written in the scriptures and as he had said he would.

# Jesus Ascends
# into Heaven

✠✠✠✠✠✠✠✠✠✠✠✠✠✠✠✠✠✠✠✠✠✠✠✠

Some time after the events in Jerusalem, Jesus did show himself to his disciples at the sea of Galilee as he had promised. The way it happened was this:

Simon Peter, with Thomas who was called the Twin, and Nathanael of Cana, and James and John the sons of Zebedee, and two others of the disciples, were together one evening on the shore of the inland sea.

Simon Peter said to the rest, "I am going fishing."

"We will go with you," said the others.

So they got into the boat and took it out into the midst of the sea. But though they lowered their net and hauled it in time and time again, they had caught nothing by the time the first dim light of dawn appeared in the sky. They turned back toward the shore with not a single fish to show for their long night's work.

At daybreak Jesus appeared on the shore. They saw him standing there in the soft and shadowy light of morning, but they did not know that it was he. As they brought the boat in toward the land he called out to them: "Children, have you any fish?"

"No," they answered with regret.

"Then cast your net on the right side of the boat, and you will find some," Jesus said.

Supposing that he was a fellow fisherman kindly offering them good advice, they cast again at once. And this time they could not haul in the net for all the multitude of fishes that it held.

Then John realized who stood upon the shore. "It is the Lord!" he said to Peter.

When Simon Peter heard that it was Jesus he quickly put on his fisherman's cloak—for he had taken it off while he worked—and sprang into the sea to go to Jesus. The other disciples followed in the boat, dragging with them the net full of fish. They were quite close to land, no more than a hundred yards away, so it was not long before they pulled the boat up on the shore. And as soon as they landed they saw a charcoal fire burning, with a fish already laid upon it, and some bread nearby. But the man whom John had said was Jesus did not look like their Lord. It puzzled them, but nevertheless they went toward him on the beach.

"Bring some of the fish which you have caught," Jesus said to them.

Simon Peter went back to the boat and hauled the net ashore. It was full of huge fish, a hundred and fifty-three of them, and even through there were so many of them the net was still unbroken.

"Come and break your fast," Jesus invited his disciples.

And though he did not look the same as he had looked before, they did not dare to ask him who he was. This time they were sure, because of the miracle of the fish, that he must be the Master.

They joined him at the fire. Jesus took the loaf of bread and gave it to them with the fish.

When they had eaten, Jesus turned to Simon Peter and said:

"Simon, son of Jona, do you love me deeply, even more than these others do?"

"Yes, Lord," Peter answered. "You know that I love you."

"Then feed my lambs for me," said Jesus. And then he asked a second time, "Simon, son of Jona, do you love me deeply?"

"Yes, Lord," Peter said again. "You know that I love you."

"Then tend my sheep for me," said Jesus. And then he asked a third time, "Simon, son of Jona, do you love me deeply?"

Peter was grieved because Jesus had asked him three times if he loved him; for he had momentarily forgotten that he had once denied his Lord three times and required his forgiveness. "Lord," he said, "you know all things. You know that I love you." But he did not understand that Jesus was speaking of divine love, a love that would sacrifice all things for his Lord.

"Then be my shepherd; feed my sheep," said Jesus. And with these words he was assuring Peter of forgiveness and entrusting him with the task of carrying on his own work. "You know that when you were young," Jesus went on, "you used to clothe yourself and go wherever you pleased. But I tell you truly that when you are old you will stretch out your hands for help, and someone else will clothe you in another way, and take you where you do not want to go." In saying this he was telling Peter that the manner of his disciple's death would not be of Peter's choosing, but that in dying as he was to die he would be glorifying God.

With these words Jesus ended their meeting. This was now the third time that Jesus had showed himself to his disciples after he had risen.

For forty days after he had risen from the dead he appeared among them many times to prove to them that he was indeed alive, and to speak to them about the kingdom of God.

One day he talked to them upon a mountainside in Galilee, and said:

"All authority in heaven and earth has been given to

me. Go, therefore, and make disciples of all the nations, baptizing them in the name of the Father, of the Son, and of the Holy Spirit. Teach them to observe all the commandments that I have given you. Preach the good news to all the world. He who believes and is baptized will be saved, but he who does not believe will be condemned. And these signs will accompany those who believe: in my name they will cast out demons; they will speak in many new tongues; they will take snakes into their hands and not be hurt; and if they drink any deadly poison, it will not harm them; they will lay hands on the sick, and the sick will recover. And I say to you that I will be with you always, even to the end of the world."

When he saw them the next time they were together in Jerusalem. And when he met with them there he commanded them to stay in Jerusalem until they received a promise from the Father. It would come in the form of a visit from the Holy Spirit, and they would know when it came that they were ready to go out and tell the gospel story.

"John baptized in water," he said, "but you will be baptized in the Holy Spirit not many days from now. You will receive power when the Holy Spirit comes upon you, and you will be my witnesses to tell the story of the truth in the city of Jerusalem, and in all Judea, and in Samaria, and to the uttermost ends of the earth. But do not leave Jerusalem until the Holy Spirit is given to you, for only then will you be ready for your work. Now let us go to Bethany, and then you must come back to the city."

So then the Lord Jesus, after he had spoken thus to them, led them out as far as Bethany.

When they were at a quiet place on the outskirts of the village he lifted up his hands and blessed them. His face was radiant and peaceful.

An unusual brightness came into the sky. And even as he blessed them he was taken up before their eyes and carried into heaven where a white cloud hid him from their sight.

And he sat down at the right hand side of God.

The disciples stood there looking upward in amazement as he disappeared. For long moments after he had gone they gazed into the heavens and wondered to themselves. And then they became aware that two men in white robes had appeared beside them.

"You men of Galilee," the strangers said to them, "why do you stand there, gazing into heaven? This same Jesus, whom you saw being taken up into heaven, will come again in the same way as you have seen him go."

Then the disciples bowed down before the wonder of it all, and they worshiped Jesus. Afterward they returned to Jerusalem with their hearts full of joy, and they spent much time in the temple praising God.

Now Jesus was gone, but his going was not the end of his story nor of his mission to the world. He left to his disciples, and to everyone on earth, a doctrine of love and a promise that he would come again. And he had also left concrete instructions for his apostles to follow. They were to wait for the promise from the Father, and then they were to go out into the world and teach what they had been taught.

While they waited they all met together with the women, including Mary the mother of Jesus, and prayed earnestly to God. And then they chose a twelfth man, Matthias, to take the place of Judas Iscariot. Now there were twelve apostles again, but many more disciples who came to join them and help them spread the word of God. Altogether there were about a hundred and twenty of them as the day of pentecost approached.

It was ten days after Jesus went to heaven that the Jews celebrated the festival of the harvest, called the feast of pentecost. On that day all the disciples gathered together to take part in the celebration.

And suddenly there came a sound from heaven, like a mighty rushing wind, and it filled all the house where they were sitting. And there appeared to them a blaze, as if of flame, that parted into tongues of fire that rested upon each one of them. All at once they were filled with the Holy Spirit, with new strength and power, and they began to speak in other languages as Jesus had said they would.

They began to preach in the temple and on the streets, and they spoke to people in the words that Jesus himself had used. When word of what had happened was noised abroad, people came to hear them from far and wide and were amazed because each man heard the disciples speak in the language which he himself understood. "Are these men not Galilaeans?" they said to one another. "Behold, they speak every language of the world!"

And it was true. The disciples spoke in many tongues, so that they could talk to all the people of the world and tell them all the glad news of the gospel. They went forth from Jerusalem with new courage and great powers, no longer afraid of the high priests and the Pharisees and determined to be Jesus' witnesses and tell the story of the truth wherever they might go. For indeed the death of Jesus was not the end; it was only the beginning.

The apostles of the Lord spread the gospel message from Jerusalem to the uttermost ends of the world: teaching, healing, suffering, gaining some enemies and many converts wherever they went. There was Peter, the rock upon whom the Christian church was founded. There was John, who carried the message far across the sea. There was Stephen, who was stoned to death for his beliefs, yet died forgiving those who killed him. There was Philip, who preached and healed in the city of Samaria. There was Paul, once a Pharisee, who became converted to Christ and taught the message of salvation in the east and in the west among the Gentiles. And there were others, more and more of them as the years passed and the story of Jesus Christ became known throughout the world. Through them the message of love and brotherhood became the new hope of the nations.

And that hope will never die.

## SIGNET and MENTOR Books of Related Interest

☐ **THE STORY BIBLE: VOLUME I by Pearl S. Buck.** The winner of the Nobel and Pulitzer Prizes retells the Greatest Story Ever Told in the living language of our times. In VOLUME I the immortal stories of the Old Testament are brought to life with a power and immediacy for the modern reader. (#W8247—$1.50)

☐ **HOW THE GREAT RELIGIONS BEGAN (revised) by Joseph Gaer.** A comparison of the differences and similarities in each religion, underscoring the spirit of brotherhood and peace that is the basic principle of all faiths. (#E7764—$1.75)

☐ **WHAT THE GREAT RELIGIONS BELIEVE by Joseph Gaer.** An enlightening account of the basic beliefs of the world's historic religions—Hinduism, Jainism, Christianity, Islam, Zoroastrianism, Confucianism, Judaism, and Zen Buddhism and others—with selections from their sacred literature. (#Y6172—$1.25)

☐ **VARIETIES OF RELIGIOUS EXPERIENCE by William James.** A new edition of James' classic work on the psychology of religion and the religious impulse. (#ME1603—$2.25)

---

**THE NEW AMERICAN LIBRARY, INC.,**
**P.O. Box 999, Bergenfield, New Jersey 07621**

Please send me the SIGNET and MENTOR BOOKS I have checked above. I am enclosing $_____(check or money order—no currency or C.O.D.'s). Please include the list price plus 35¢ a copy to cover handling and mailing costs. (Prices and numbers are subject to change without notice.)

Name_____

Address_____

City_____State_____Zip Code_____
Allow at least 4 weeks for delivery

# MENTOR Books on Religion

☐ **THE LIVING TALMUD: The Wisdom of the Fathers and Its Classical Commentaries selected and translated by Judah Goldin.** A new translation, with an illuminating essay on the place of the Talmud in Jewish life and religion. (#ME1669—$1.75)

☐ **HERE I STAND: A LIFE OF MARTIN LUTHER by Roland H. Bainton.** A vivid portrait of Martin Luther, the man who, because of his unshakable faith in his God, helped to establish the Protestant religion. (#ME1580—$1.75)

☐ **THE MEANING OF THE DEAD SEA SCROLLS by A. Powell Davies.** A fascinating interpretation of one of the most important archaeological discoveries of recent times; the finding of ancient documents which revolutionize religious teachings and beliefs.
(#MW1502—$1.50)

☐ **THE MEANING OF THE GLORIOUS KORAN: An Explanatory Translation by Mohammed Marmaduke Pickthall.** The complete sacred book of Mohammedanism, translated with reference to scholarship. (#ME1652—$2.50)

☐ **THE SAYINGS OF CONFUCIUS translated by James R. Ware.** A new translation of the sayings of the greatest wise man of ancient China, teaching the ageless virtues of civilized men. (#MY1557—$1.25)

---